Pastability

Pastability
Lizzie Spender

Illustrations by
Karen Kerridge

THE ECCO PRESS
NEW YORK

Copyright © 1987 by Lizzie Spender

First published in 1988 by The Ecco Press
26 West 17th Street, New York, NY 10011

Published by arrangement with Faber and Faber, Ltd.

Printed in the United States of America

Library of Congress Cataloging-in-Publication Data

Spender, Lizzie.
Pastability.

Reprint. Originally published:
London: Faber and Faber, 1987.
Includes index.
1. Cookery (Macaroni)   I. Title.
TX809.M17S64   1988   641.8'22   88-11051

ISBN 0-88001-201-3

To Annie Brown

Contents

Types and shapes of pasta · Alternative pasta · How to
cook pasta · Fresh pasta · Which type of pasta? · How
to serve pasta · Pasta as an accompaniment ·
Leftovers · Improvisation · Standby ingredients ·
Health, diet and pasta · Pasta and weight control ·
Equipment · Metric weights and measures · Béchamel
sauce

Meatless dishes

Dishes without dairy products

Meat dishes

Fish dishes

Acknowledgements

I would like to thank the following people. My friend Walter Donohue who suggested I turn the idea into a book. Giuseppe Tomé who gave me good advice about many things especially cooking pasta. All my loyal friends who valiantly ate vast quantities of pasta with nothing but startling enthusiasm. They will know who they are, but they include in particular Derek Marlowe, Mossa Bildner, David Meredith, Michael Pennington, Johnny Gaynor, Philip Cayford, Walter Donohue, Annie and Gardner Brown, Stephen and Natasha Spender, Lord and Lady Moyne and their family, Gerald and Camilla Harford, and Peter, Patrick, Tamsin and Alice Jay.

I would like to thank those friends who suggested ideas for recipes, most of whom I have written about in the recipe itself, but in addition, Elizabeth Roberti, Virginia Zervudachi, Maria Teresa Gavazzi, Michael Conroy, Henry Wyndham and Charles Mitchener.

Francesa and Idelma who taught me at a very early age to look to the pasta pot for one of the good things in life.

Sainsbury, Waitrose, Safeways, Buitoni, Marks and Spencer and Barilla for providing information and samples.

Lastly a very special thanks to Kate Fletcher who bravely took on the job of typing out my manuscript. I am deeply grateful for her invaluable assistance, advice and encouragement.

Lizzie Spender

Pastability

Introduction

TYPES AND SHAPES OF PASTA

There is an Italian name for every pasta shape and type, but only a few of these names are widely used outside Italy. To avoid confusion, and to help make shopping for pasta problem-free, I have used the Italian name only if a pasta is generally known by that name (e.g. tagliatelle). Otherwise, for pastas you would usually buy under an English name (e.g. shells), I have given the English name in the recipes.

The following is a list of the pastas I have used in this book with their Italian names and English equivalents where appropriate, and is included as a guide should you come across the Italian for a pasta which I have named in English.

Italian	English
cannelloni	
conchiglie	shells
farfalle	bows, butterflies
fettuccine	ribbon noodles
fusilli	twists
lasagne	
linguine	
maccheroni	macaroni, pasta tubes
penne	quills
rigatoni	ribbed pasta tubes
spaghetti	
spaghettini	
tagliatelle	ribbon noodles

ALTERNATIVE PASTA

I like to use the various coloured pastas now widely available: the green (which is basically a durum wheat semolina pasta tinted by the addition of spinach) and the red–orange (tinted by the addition of tomato, or very occasionally pumpkin). I have never been struck by any great difference in taste, but they do look pretty, particularly combined with the less colourful pasta sauces such as 'crab cream'. Best of all are the packets of pasta in all three colours, red, yellow and green.

Buckwheat spaghetti, available in health food shops, is *very* delicious but be warned, it is also more expensive. It has a distinctive and delicate flavour of its own, which I find combines well with the simpler sauces, for example the oil, garlic and herb sauces and the vegetable sauces without cream or cheese.

The wholewheat pastas combine well with everything, but in particular the vegetable sauces and those with cream and cheese. Both the buckwheat and the wholewheat need careful attention and a little practice when cooking in order to catch them at the 'al dente' stage. In general, wholewheat will take a little longer to cook than the equivalent shape in white durum wheat semolina.

HOW TO COOK PASTA

How much to cook?

The amount of pasta you need to cook will of course vary with the appetites of those who are going to eat it. In the recipes I have given quantities for quite generous servings. When estimating quantities, work on the basis of 3–4 ounces (75–125 grammes) dried pasta, or 4–6 ounces (100–175 grammes) fresh pasta, for an average-sized main course helping.

How much water?

It is important to cook the pasta in *plenty* of boiling water, otherwise it will have a glutinous, starchy quality. I recommend you use the following table as a guide to quantities:

Pasta		Water	
ounces	grammes	pints	litres
Up to 4 oz	Up to 125 g	$1\frac{1}{2}$–2	1
4	125	2	1–$1\frac{1}{2}$
8	225	4	$2\frac{1}{2}$
16	450	8	$4\frac{1}{2}$
24	675	12	7
32	900	16	9

I possess one medium-size pan (4 pints) in which I cook 1–2 main course servings, and a couple of huge pans (16 pints) in which I cook larger quantities using whatever quantity of water is necessary.

To cook the pasta

First add to the water 1 teaspoon (1 × 5 ml spoon) of salt per 4 oz (100–125 g) pasta and ½–1 teaspoon (0.5–1 × 5 ml spoon) oil – cheap vegetable oil will do. Bring the water to a fast boil before adding the pasta, otherwise you will increase the tendency for the pieces to stick together. Throw in the pasta *all at once*, and immediately stir well with a wooden spoon to separate the pieces. It is at this point that the pasta is in danger of congealing, so make sure the pieces are moving freely.

Cook until 'al dente', that is, done but still firm (not hard) to the bite. It takes practice to know when pasta is ready. Even now, I still almost always ask for a second opinion. It is almost impossible to predict how long a particular pasta will take to cook, which is why I have not given cooking times in the recipes. Thick, solid pieces, such as large pasta tubes or shells, will obviously take much longer than a fine spaghetti, but it is very dangerous to try to invent any rules of thumb as there are too many variables. Don't rely on the packet to give you the correct cooking time. Getting it right is really a matter of standing over the pan, and when the pasta is nearly ready, tasting every 45 seconds until it is. Pasta can overcook in just a matter of seconds, especially one that is not made from 100 per cent durum wheat semolina. I do *not* believe the old adage 'Throw a piece of spaghetti at the wall and if it sticks the pasta is ready'. In my experience, it all depends on how sticky your kitchen walls are!

When the pasta is 'al dente', drain it immediately into a colander standing in the sink. Then pick up the colander with its contents and shake it well to remove excess water before returning the pasta to the saucepan or a preheated serving dish.

Timing your cooking

For most dishes the pasta and the sauce should be cooked simultaneously, so that the pasta is ready with the sauce. You will soon learn how to synchronize them but don't despair if you don't. For most dishes it is possible to keep the sauce waiting as long as it is reheated gently while you are draining the pasta – and is served hot. If the pasta is cooked before you are ready to mix in the sauce, stir in a teaspoon of olive oil or a knob of butter. Mix in the sauce as soon as possible and serve immediately.

Aim to time your cooking so that the sauce is ready a little before the pasta, as waiting pasta can easily overcook and congeal. If you do find yourself in trouble, throw a little oil on the pasta and reheat it *with the sauce.*

Occasionally, especially when entertaining friends, you may prefer to make the sauce well in advance. Reheat gently, and bear in mind you may need to add a little more liquid at the last minute.

Precooking lasagne and cannelloni

Cooking lasagne and cannelloni tubes is tricky. It's very easy to end up with burnt fingers and the pasta on the floor, or with a mass of congealed lasagne leaves impossible to separate. Many people swear by the 'oven-ready' type and a few are brave enough to use the traditional kind without precooking. When I have tried using unprecooked lasagne or cannelloni it has always been slightly too glutinous for my taste, and has taken a *long* time to cook in the oven. But it is worth trying the 'oven-ready' type. Here are two tips for cooking it: make sure there is plenty of very liquid sauce for the pasta to absorb; and cover the whole dish tightly with kitchen foil for at least the first half of the cooking time – this will help the lasagne absorb the liquid.

To precook lasagne and cannelloni (my method)

First fill a large saucepan with 3–4 inches (8–10 cm) of water, and add ½ teaspoon (1 × 2.5 ml spoon) salt and ½ teaspoon (1 × 2.5 ml spoon) oil. Bring the water to a fast boil before slipping in the lasagne leaves (or cannelloni tubes) three at a time, stirring well with a wooden spoon to separate them. After 2–3 minutes, when the pasta is still very 'al dente' (i.e slightly undercooked), remove the pieces one by one using a slotted spoon and the wooden spoon – and taking care not to let the pasta slip out of your grip! Dip each leaf or tube into a shallow bowl containing

4

cold water and a couple of tablespoons of oil. Then put to one side on a board, spread out and overlapped like a deck of cards.

I have found the best way to make lasagne or cannelloni dishes is to prepare the sauce before cooking the pasta. I can then lay the precooked pasta in the baking dish as soon as it is removed from the boiling water, adding the sauce as I go. This method avoids all the fiddly business of rinsing the pasta in cold water and spreading it on a flat surface.

FRESH PASTA

I have not included a recipe for fresh pasta in this book as I believe the genuine article requires special equipment and a good deal of patience, and I possess neither. For my pasta cooking I prefer to rely on a good dried brand with the occasional indulgence in excellent homemade pasta.

I tend to be a little suspicious of some of the so-called fresh pastas now widely available, even those sold by the new pasta shops that have sprung up all over the place in the last few years. The pre-packaged varieties are often a pasteurized version – not surprisingly, as true fresh pasta lasts such a short time – and some of the trendy new shops are known to use the wrong kind of soft flour and to make the pasta with incorrect machinery. The softer flour is not only less nutritious but also produces a pasta difficult to cook and, in my experience, almost impossible to serve 'al dente'. A further drawback to using fresh pasta is that it is more expensive than dried pasta.

My advice is to try out local shops (especially an old-fashioned Italian delicatessen if you are lucky enough to live or work near one) and if you find a shop that produces a fresh pasta which is truly more delicious and as easy to cook as a good dried brand, stick to it!

Storing and cooking fresh pasta

Genuine fresh pasta keeps in the fridge for two or three days. It is possible to freeze it – in which case it keeps for up to six months – and to cook it directly from the freezer. For tagliatelle or spaghetti I would recommend the following method of freezing. Spread the pasta out flat on a plate (or plates) to a

5

thickness of not more than an inch or so (about 3 cm). Put the plate and pasta into a plastic bag and freeze. When the pasta is frozen, remove the plate, seal the pasta into the plastic bag, and return it to the deep freeze. If you freeze the pasta as a solid mass in a bag, when the time comes to cook it there is a danger the outside strands will be 'al dente' while the centre of the lump is still completely frozen.

Fresh pasta takes considerably less time to cook than dried. It is dangerous to try to predict how long, as all pasta is different. Count on a third to a half of the time the equivalent dried pasta would take, or count on less than 3 minutes – and a maximum of 5. Watch it like a hawk as it can overcook in a matter of seconds, particularly if it is made with soft flour.

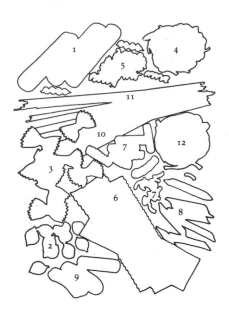

1 cannelloni	7 macaroni
2 conchiglie	8 penne
3 farfalle	9 rigatoni
4 fettuccine	10 spaghetti
5 fusilli	11 spaghettini
6 lasagne	12 tagliatelle

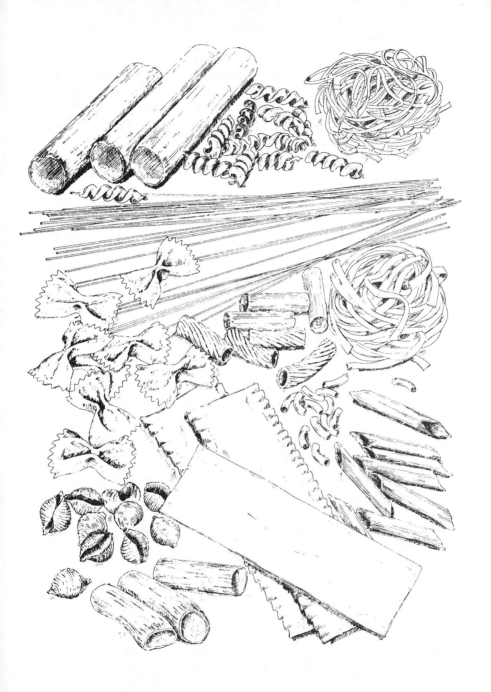

WHICH TYPE OF PASTA?

The types of pasta I have suggested are those which are most readily available in the shops, and for each recipe I have suggested a type or types I know from experience will go well with that particular sauce. Of course, you do not have to use the pasta I have specified – you can substitute one type for another according to your own preference and what is to hand.

With Italian cooking there are traditional combinations of pasta type and sauce which are probably more consistently adhered to in restaurants than in private houses. There are also wonderful theories which I have heard discussed more frequently in America than in Italy: that the simple oil sauce clings best to the pasta strand, such as spaghetti and linguine; that the shell-like shapes scoop up a semi-liquid sauce; that the meat with oil sauce – the bolognese ragu – sticks to the ridges of the ribbed, tubular rigatoni. The twists, I suppose, do a bit of everything. Remember that a heavy pasta is the best complement to a heavy sauce.

HOW TO SERVE PASTA

It is essential with most pasta dishes that they be served *very* hot, and as soon as they are ready. It is therefore advisable to round up those about to eat the pasta and persuade them to sit at the table just *before* the dish is actually ready! Plates should be well warmed in advance, and it is important, if you are intending to transfer the pasta from the pan to a serving dish, to preheat the dish too.

If you plan to serve grated cheese on the side, I would recommend suggesting to people that they try the pasta before adding cheese. I find that if cheese is on the table, people automatically add it without tasting first to see if the dish really needs it.

PASTA AS AN ACCOMPANIMENT

Pasta makes an excellent accompaniment to almost any main course dish and, in particular, to anything with a sauce, be it meat, fish or vegetarian. Use it whenever you would normally use potatoes. (If you are using fresh pasta, the timing will be tricky, especially if you are also juggling with the main course and possibly a vegetable.) All you really need to put on the pasta is a little butter, oil or cream, and seasoning, but you could embellish it with, for example, some mushrooms fried in butter, some grated cheese, or a little broccoli or courgette. My mother adds a sprinkling of anis seeds to lightly buttered tagliatelle and serves it with a creamy veal stew or chicken breasts prepared with a light sauce.

LEFTOVERS

Make the most of leftovers – cold vegetables, scraps of meat or chicken, ends of cheese, sauces from stews and casseroles. All can be utilized in the concoction of delicious, original pasta sauces.

Leftover cold pasta can always be used the next day. Some dishes taste excellent cold. Others can be heated up as follows. Add a little liquid – chicken stock, cream, white wine, oil, butter, or combinations of these – and warm gently in a pan, stirring with a wooden spoon and adding more liquid if necessary. Another possibility is to mix in some béchamel sauce, sprinkle grated cheese on top and bake in the oven. Last but not least is a dish famous in Italy, 'Spaghetti omelette' (see page 21) or, my variation, 'Pasta scrambled egg' (see page 20).

IMPROVISATION

Do improvise. I think half the point of cooking with pasta is to be able to make the sauce with whatever ingredients are easily available. My recipe ingredients are, in a sense, only suggestions. There is practically no ingredient (apart from the pasta itself and a little butter, oil or liquid) which cannot be omitted or substituted for another. I make pasta sauces with whatever I find in the fridge or larder, or whatever looks fresh and is a good buy in the shops. I consider it a creative challenge to be presented with somebody else's fridge or cupboard – however bare – and asked to concoct a pasta dish.

STANDBY INGREDIENTS

If you keep a selection of dried pastas and some basic sauce ingredients you will be able to throw together a pasta meal at short notice and without a quick dash to the shops. The following list includes all the basic standbys, with items I regard as absolutely essential marked with an asterisk.

The storecupboard

*tinned Italian plum tomatoes (Ciro is recommended by my
   Italian friends, but Waitrose, Safeways and Sainsbury's
   brands are also good)
*tomato purée (available in tubes, jars or tins – to be kept in the
   fridge once opened. Transfer remaining contents of a tin to
   another receptacle)
 tins of fish: *anchovies; salmon; sardines; *tuna fish; clams;
   crab; mussels (but not those preserved in a vinegary liquid)
 olives and capers
*chicken stock cubes (or vegetable cubes if you are vegetarian)
*garlic
 dried red chillies; chilli powder
*dried herbs (especially marjoram, oregano, sage, thyme, basil)
*sea salt
*whole black peppercorns
 longlife cream
 pesto sauce (the jar should be kept in the fridge after it has been
   opened)
 wine
*good olive oil (It is important to use good quality oil as the oil
   used affects the taste of so many of the recipes. I would buy a
   big bottle or tin of Italian or Greek oil. Bought in quantity the
   oil will probably work out not too expensive, and certainly it
   will be more delicious than oil from one of those dubious
   plastic bottles, tiny and very expensive, which are
   optimistically labelled 'olive oil'. Sometimes you can pick up a
   bargain in the way of a big, reasonably priced bottle at a local
   corner store run by Greeks, Italians or Indians. I find the oils
   which are strong yellow, or even green in colour, to be the
   most flavoursome.)
*Pasta (A selection of packets of your favourite brand of pasta, in
   different shapes and types. I prefer the make F. lli de Cecco di
   Filippo, recognizable by its bright turquoise and yellow
   packets. It is available in Italian delicatessens, and I make a
   point of stocking up whenever I find it. I also use and highly
   recommend Barilla, which is more easily available. Whatever
   the brand, always use a pasta which is made from 100 per cent
   durum wheat semolina. It will not only be more nutritious
   than a pasta made with a softer flour, or a mixture of flours,

but will also be easier to cook. It will remain at the 'al dente' stage for a little longer, thus lessening the hazard of your perfectly cooked pasta turning into a congealed and soggy mess somewhere between draining and serving.)

The fridge

 eggs
 single and double cream
*butter
 bacon
 fresh vegetables
*fresh, ungrated Parmesan cheese and/or fresh Cheddar cheese
*onions (Do experiment with the unusual varieties if you come
    across them – the little shallots for example, or the large,
    dark-red onion.)

The freezer

If you have a freezer, I would recommend storing a selection of the following items:
chicken breasts
chicken livers
minced meat
prawns
leaf spinach
peas
broad beans

Parmesan cheese

Parmesan is best bought in a lump and kept wrapped in paper in the fridge. It must not be covered in clingfilm or foil: if it cannot breathe it will go mouldy. Stored this way the cheese should keep for months, so it is well worth buying a decent-sized piece when the opportunity arises. Buying Parmesan can be a painful experience, for it is expensive. Console yourself with the fact that a little goes a long way. It is not really worth bothering with the little packets and round boxes of ready-grated Parmesan: the stuff is often tasteless and always expensive – and does *not* go a long way.

Grate the Parmesan as and when you need it. Quite often I leave a lump of Parmesan with a grater on a plate on the table.

This is not only economical, but it discourages people from the deplorable habit of throwing a spoon of Parmesan on to the pasta before they have tasted the dish and decided whether or not that particular dish needs it. Parmesan has a strong flavour and can drown the delicate taste of some dishes.

Tomato cartons

Many shops now stock cartons of tomatoes. Those I have tried resemble a combination of tinned tomatoes and concentrated tomato purée, and are quite acceptable. Use one carton (500 g) to replace one 14 oz (400 g) tin of tomatoes. If you use carton tomatoes, taste the sauce before adding tomato purée as you may find the flavour is strong enough without.

HEALTH, DIET AND PASTA

As we all know, and are constantly reminded by the media, ideas on what constitutes a healthy diet have changed radically over the last ten or so years. The 'meat and two veg' and 'more protein the better' scheme of things has been replaced by the low cholesterol, high fibre, balanced diet, with the emphasis on fresh ingredients – especially vegetables and fruit – and the avoidance of chemical additives.

As it happens, pasta fits in very well with these views, especially when served with low animal fat sauces – those containing oil and plenty of fresh vegetables, or maybe a little fish. For those supremely cholesterol-conscious, it would be advisable to avoid all animal fats and to replace the oil with a vegetable oil. Those who are fibre-conscious can concentrate on the vegetable sauces and replace the ordinary durum wheat semolina pasta with the wholewheat varieties.

All the recipes in the first section, 'Meatless dishes', are suitable for a vegetarian diet (substituting vegetable stock or water for chicken stock, where used). The recipes on pages 52–70 contain no animal products – cheese on the side, where suggested, is, of course, never an essential.

PASTA AND WEIGHT CONTROL

It is a fallacy that pasta is fattening although, like any food, it is fattening if you eat too much of it. The pasta itself, uncooked, is about 100 calories an ounce (about 25 grammes). Cooked, it is about 33 calories. Weight for weight, it is considerably lower in calories than, say, grilled red meat.

Obviously, if you choose to make sauces full of double cream, cheese, butter and oil, they will prove more fattening than sauces made with tomatoes or other fresh vegetables and a small amount of oil or butter. On the whole, I have kept the quantities of oil and butter as low as possible, often substituting a liquid such as chicken stock. An Italian would be inclined to be far more generous than I have been with the olive oil.

It is actually possible to lose weight on pasta, and to keep it off. I've done it myself, following a calorie-controlled diet. For those wishing to follow suit I have included a few low-calorie dishes (pages 17, 65, 66). Determined weight watchers could adapt the ingredients for many of the other recipes – or buy a calorie counter and invent their own dishes.

EQUIPMENT

The essential basic equipment necessary for cooking pasta dishes is minimal. A large saucepan in which to cook the pasta itself (*very* large if you are intending to entertain more than four or five people), and a large colander for draining it; a medium-sized frying pan and medium-sized saucepan for preparing sauces; a couple of wooden spoons for stirring (and possibly serving) the pasta and sauce; a large bowl or plate, which can be preheated, for serving the pasta at table; a couple of ovenproof dishes or pans for cooking lasagnes and other baked pasta dishes; and a cheese grater, a garlic squeezer and a sharp knife for chopping meat and vegetables.

METRIC WEIGHTS AND MEASURES

In all the recipes I have given both imperial and metric weights and measures – but not in exact conversions. Rather, for ease of measuring in grammes and millilitres, I have given conversions from imperial to metric in units of 25. Where an exact conversion lies midway between two such units, I have indicated this by giving the units below and above the precise conversion. *For example*: 3 ounces converts to approximately 85 grammes, and would be shown as 75–100 grammes in the recipes.

13

The one exception to this principle is ½ ounce which throughout has been given as 15 grammes.

BÉCHAMEL SAUCE

Béchamel sauce is used in a number of the recipes. Rather than repeat the instructions for making it each time it occurs, I have given the basic recipe at the end of the book (page 144) and included the quantities needed for individual recipes in the ingredients lists.

Meatless dishes

COOKING AND SERVING PASTA

Choice of pasta

You don't have to use the pasta type specified in a particular recipe, but if you want to use another type bear in mind that as a general rule it is best to substitute one pasta type with another of similar characteristics (see page 8).

Timing

The time needed for pasta to cook can vary so much that I have not specified cooking times in the recipes. Aim to have the pasta ready at the same time as the sauce, and test it frequently as it nears the 'al dente' stage (see pages 2–4).

Serve it *hot*!

Hot pasta dishes should be served while they are still *very* hot. Always preheat plates and serving dishes.

'Cheese on the side'

Not all pasta dishes are improved by adding grated cheese. Serve it as a side dish to be added only if needed – *after* tasting.

Wholewheat pasta shells with vegetables

Most vegetables, especially the green leafy kinds, are comparatively low in calories and high in fibre. A dish made up of a high proportion of green vegetables, some pasta and a very little fat will be both substantial and surprisingly 'non-fattening'. The quantities given for this recipe are sufficient for three strict dieters (250 calories per portion), or two less strict (370 calories per portion) – or for one dieter and one person who isn't counting calories. You could even add butter and extra cheese to the double-size non-diet portion.

(Broccoli works well with this recipe, but you could use other vegetables, alone or in combination. Try spinach, leeks, carrots, or mushrooms with spinach.)

For 3 diet portions, use:

>   8 oz (225 g) Brussels sprouts (weighed after preparation)
>   8 oz (225 g) broccoli (weighed after preparation)
>   4 oz (100–125 g) cottage cheese
>   1–2 cloves garlic, crushed
>   salt and pepper
>   1 tablespoon (1 × 15 ml spoon) grated Parmesan cheese
>   5 oz (150 g) wholewheat pasta shells (or other pasta shape)

Wash the Brussels sprouts, removing the outer leaves and the ends of the stalks. Cut the larger sprouts into halves and quarters. Wash the broccoli, cut off the ends of the stalks, then slice the broccoli into ½-inch (1-cm) pieces.

In a small bowl mix the cottage cheese with the crushed garlic, salt, pepper and grated Parmesan cheese. Put aside.

Steam the vegetables until they are softened, but still with some 'bite' (about a couple of minutes). (I use a small metal steamer placed inside a saucepan with a well-fitting lid.) Then drain the vegetables and replace them in the saucepan, covered but without the steamer, to keep warm.

Meanwhile, cook the pasta in plenty of salted, boiling water. Drain, and return to the pan. Add the vegetables and the cottage cheese mixture to the pasta, and turn all the ingredients with a wooden spoon over a low heat until well heated through.

Serve immediately.

Spinach and wholewheat macaroni bake

For 2 main course helpings, use:

½ oz (15 g) butter
1 tablespoon (1 × 15 ml spoon) olive oil
1 clove garlic, crushed
4 oz (100–125 g) onion, sliced
8 oz (225 g) wholewheat small macaroni (or other small
   pasta shape)
8 oz (225 g) frozen spinach, *or* 12 oz (325–350 g) fresh
   spinach
2 eggs, beaten
grated nutmeg (to taste)
salt and pepper
4 oz (100–125 g) Cheddar cheese, grated
8 oz (225 g) cottage cheese

In a large pan, gently sauté the garlic and onion in the oil and
butter over a low heat until translucent. Remove from the heat.
Meanwhile, cook the pasta in plenty of boiling, salted water
until 'al dente'. Drain and put aside.

Cook the spinach, according to the instructions on the packet
if it is frozen. If using fresh spinach, wash the leaves thoroughly
to remove any grit, then boil in a *very little* (about ½ a teacup)
lightly salted water, drain well and chop coarsely. Add the
spinach to the pan with the onions and garlic. Sauté together for
a couple of minutes before removing the pan from the heat and
stirring in the cooked macaroni, cottage cheese, nutmeg,
seasoning, 2 oz (50 g) of the Cheddar cheese, and finally the
beaten eggs. (The eggs must go in last to prevent any danger of
them scrambling in the hot spinach and onion mixture.)

Pour the mixture into an ovenproof dish, sprinkle the
remaining 2 oz (50 g) grated cheese on the top, and bake in a
preheated oven (375°F/190°C/gas mark 5) for 30–45 minutes.

Serve hot.

Pasta scrambled eggs

A delicious way to use up leftover pasta.

For 2 main course helpings, use:

> 2 eggs (3 if the pasta is very dry)
> herbs to taste (additional to those in the sauce)
> 2 oz (50 g) grated Cheddar, Parmesan (or other hard cheese)
> 1 oz (25 g) butter, *or* 2 tablespoons (2 × 15 ml spoons) oil
> 10–12 oz (275–350 g) leftover pasta and sauce
> salt and pepper

Beat the eggs together with the herbs, grated cheese and seasoning. Stir the mixture into the leftover pasta and sauce. Heat the butter in a large pan. When it begins to bubble, add the egg and pasta mixture and cook over a medium heat, stirring continuously with a wooden spoon until the eggs have scrambled.
Serve very hot.

Note: If the pasta looks a little dry and boring, you could add an extra ingredient or two: some sautéd onions or garlic for example, some mushrooms gently fried in butter, or some skinned and coarsely chopped tomatoes – or perhaps even a little cream and some chopped, fried bacon.

Spaghetti omelette

This is an Italian version of Spanish omelette. Although it is called 'spaghetti' omelette, it can of course be made with virtually any sort of pasta. If it does not want to turn into an omelette, concede gracefully and turn it into 'Pasta scrambled eggs' (page 20). As with that recipe, if the pasta looks a little dry (if, perhaps, at a previous meal people have taken all the sauce with their servings and left virtually plain cooked pasta as leftovers!) then add an extra ingredient or two (see page 20).

For 2 main course helpings, use:

> 6 oz (175 g) leftover spaghetti (or other pasta) with remaining sauce
> 3 eggs (4 if the pasta is very dry)
> 2 oz (50 g) grated Cheddar (or other hard cheese)
> herbs and spices to taste (in addition to those already in the sauce)
> salt and pepper
> 1½ oz (25–50 g) butter, *or* 3 tablespoons (3 × 15 ml spoons) oil

Beat the eggs together with the herbs, grated cheese and seasoning. Stir into the pasta. Heat half the butter in a large frying pan over a medium heat, then pour in the mixture, loosening the edges with a spatula or fish slice. When you guess the underside is cooked, remove the pan from the heat and loosen the bottom of the omelette with a fish slice. Place a large plate (just larger than the frying pan) face down over the pan and flip the omelette, cooked side up, on to the plate. Carry out this delicate operation over a very clean stretch of kitchen surface so that if there are any accidents you can rescue the omelette. (If you are not feeling brave enough to turn the omelette, you can place the frying pan under the grill to cook the top side of the omelette.)

Clean out any burnt bits from the pan, then heat the remaining butter in it. Slide the omelette back into the pan and cook the remaining side as before.

Serve hot.

A movable vegetarian feast

A few months ago I made a lunch for an old friend, the film director John Huston, during one of his visits to London. The lunch was a glorious, informal reunion of his children, grandchildren, unofficially adopted children (such as myself) and a couple of very close friends, Eve Arnold the photographer and the producer Michael Fitzgerald. The brief was: the dish must travel in the back of my car to the apartment where he was staying, to be cooked quickly using any available equipment. It must be light and delicate for John, vegetarian for his youngest son Danny and Danny's mother Zoë, appeal to children from the age of two upwards, be delicious, filling, and feed any number from ten to fourteen people!

As it was a buffet lunch I served pasta quills. Attempting to twirl spaghetti or tagliatelle on to a fork from a plate on your knee can all too easily result in sauce on the carpet or all over your clothes.

For 8–10 main course helpings, use:

> 1 lb (450 g) broad beans (frozen – or use frozen peas or
>   french beans)
> 4 oz (100–125 g) butter
> 2 cloves garlic, crushed
> 6 oz (175 g) onion, sliced
> 3 large courgettes, sliced
> 1½ pints (850 ml) single cream
> 2¼ lb (1 kg approx.) tomatoes, skinned and coarsely
>   chopped
> 1 Mozzarella cheese (5 oz/150 g) (or another semi-hard
>   cheese)
> 6 oz (175 g) Gruyère or Emmenthal cheese
> salt and pepper
> 2¼ lb (1 kg approx.) quills (or any other short, tubular pasta
>   shape)

Cook the beans for a couple of minutes in a little salted, boiling water. Drain and put aside.

Gently sauté the garlic and onion in the butter until softened and translucent. Add the courgettes and continue to sauté for a few minutes. Add the cream and the beans, and continue to cook on a low heat for about 5 minutes, stirring frequently. At the last moment add the tomatoes and cheese and cook just until the sauce is heated through. Season.

Cook the pasta in plenty of salted, boiling water until 'al dente'. Drain, and put back into the pot or into a preheated serving dish. Pour on the sauce (reheated if necessary) and stir together well.

Serve immediately.

Spinach lasagne

For 6 main course helpings, use:

For the spinach filling

>2 lb (900–925 g) spinach
>1½ oz (25–50 g) butter
>2 cloves garlic, crushed
>12 oz (325–350 g) cottage cheese
>2 egg yolks
>grated rind of 1 large lemon (or 1½ small lemons)
>¾ teaspoon (1½ × 2.5 ml spoons) grated nutmeg
>4 oz (100–125 g) grated Cheddar cheese
>salt and pepper

For the béchamel sauce

>1½ oz (25–50 g) butter
>1½ oz (25–50 g) flour
>1 pint (575 ml) milk
>½ teaspoon (1 × 2.5 ml spoon) mustard powder

Additional ingredients

>salt and pepper
>1 lb (450 g) lasagne
>6 oz (175 g) grated Cheddar cheese

If you are using frozen spinach, defrost it in a little boiling, salted water. Strain, pushing the spinach against the strainer or colander to remove as much liquid as possible. If the spinach is fresh, cook it in a very little milk, strain, and chop coarsely. Add the milk to the milk for the béchamel sauce.

Melt the butter in the bottom of a large saucepan on a very low heat. Add the garlic, and almost immediately add the spinach, sautéing for a few minutes on the low heat. Put to one side. Mix together the cottage cheese, egg yolks, lemon rind, nutmeg, Cheddar cheese and seasoning, and add to the cooled spinach. Mix all the ingredients together well.

Make a béchamel sauce with the ingredients stated, following the instructions on page 144.

Cook the lasagne as instructed on pages 4–5.

Take a fairly shallow ovenproof dish (3–4 inches/7.5–10 cm deep) and butter it well. Spread a layer of the spinach mixture very sparsely on the bottom of the dish. Spread a couple of large spoonsful of béchamel sauce over it, then add some grated cheese and seasoning. Follow with a layer of lasagne, overlapping the edges slightly. Repeat the process until you run out of ingredients, ending with some béchamel sauce on top of the last layer of lasagne, and a generous sprinkling of Cheddar cheese.

Cover the dish with foil, and bake in a fairly hot oven (400°F/200°C/gas mark 6) for 1–1½ hours. Remove the foil for the last 15–20 minutes to allow the cheese topping to brown.

Carrot, courgette, leek and mushroom lasagne

This dish is delicious – fresh but substantial. You could serve it at a dinner party where some or all of your guests are vegetarian.

For 6 main course helpings, use:

For the carrot and leek filling

>	1 oz (25 g) butter
>	2 tablespoons (2 × 15 ml spoons) olive oil
>	4 oz (100–125 g) onion, finely sliced
>	1 clove garlic, crushed
>	1 lb (450 g) carrots, finely sliced or chopped
>	8 oz (225 g) leeks, finely sliced
>	3 tablespoons (3 × 15 ml spoons) fruit juice (apple or orange)
>	¼ pint (150 ml) chicken or vegetable stock, *or* hot water

For the courgette and mushroom filling

>	1 oz (25 g) butter
>	2 tablespoons (2 × 15 ml spoons) olive oil
>	4 oz (100–125 g) onion, finely sliced
>	1 clove garlic, crushed
>	12 oz (325–350 g) mushrooms, sliced
>	12 oz (325–350 g) courgettes, finely sliced
>	¼ pint (150 ml) chicken or vegetable stock, or hot water

For the béchamel sauce

>	1 oz (25 g) butter
>	1 oz (25 g) flour
>	1 pint (575 ml) milk
>	1 teaspoon (1 × 5 ml spoon) dry mustard powder

Additional ingredients

> ¼ pint (150 ml) single cream
> 4 oz (100–125 g) shelled walnuts
> 8 oz (225 g) grated Cheddar cheese
> salt and pepper
> 11–18 oz (300–500 g) lasagne (see pages 4–5.)

Take 2 large saucepans with lids and start cooking the carrot
and courgette fillings simultaneously. In each pan sauté the
onion and garlic in the oil and butter on a very low heat,
removing the lid to stir occasionally, until the onion is quite
mushy. (Alternatively, leave them both in the oven at
275°F/140°C/gas mark 1 for 30 minutes, stirring occasionally.)

Add the sliced mushrooms to one of the pans, stirring well
over a low heat to allow them to absorb the juices. After 2–3
minutes add the courgettes, and then the stock. Replace the
lid and leave to simmer, stirring occasionally, for about
15 minutes.

Add the leeks to the other pan of onion mixture, stirring well
over a gentle heat for a few minutes. Then add the carrots and
fruit juice. After a couple of minutes add the stock and leave to
simmer, covered, for a further 15 minutes.

Make a thin béchamel sauce following the instructions on
page 144.

Cook the lasagne following the instructions on
pages 4–5.

Take a flat ovenproof dish, 3–4 inches (7½–10 cms) deep, and
butter it well. (I use an earthenware oval dish about 15 inches
(38 cms) × 10 inches (25 cms) × 2½ inches (6 cms). Spread a thin
layer of the carrot filling over the bottom so that it barely hides
the base. Spread over it a couple of tablespoons of béchamel
sauce, sprinkle on some Cheddar cheese, and then lay a layer of
lasagne with the strips just overlapping at the edges. Then
spread a layer each of the courgette filling, béchamel and
cheese, followed by a layer of lasagne. Continue this way until
all the ingredients are used up (I aim for about 2 layers of each
filling), ending with a layer of lasagne on which you spread a
fairly generous dollop of béchamel sauce.

Pour the cream all over the top, and sprinkle on the nuts and a
handful of grated cheese. Cover with foil so that the pasta will

absorb some of the juices, and cook in a hot oven (400°F/200°C/gas mark 6) for 1–1½ hours depending on when you are ready to eat, removing the foil for the last 15–30 minutes to allow the dish to brown.

Spinach cannelloni

For 8–10 main course helpings, use:

For the spinach filling

    1 oz (25 g) butter
    2 tablespoons (2 × 15 ml spoons) olive oil
    10 oz (275 g) onion, sliced
    2 cloves garlic, crushed
    *1½ lb (675 g) frozen spinach (defrosted)
    2 eggs
    2 fl oz (50 ml) single cream
    1 oz (25 g) flour
    salt and pepper
    grated nutmeg to taste (I use ⅛–¼ of a whole nutmeg)
    grated rind of 1 lemon
    1 oz (25 g) grated Parmesan, *or* 2 oz (50 g) Emmenthal or
        Cheddar cheese
    12 oz (325–350 g) cottage cheese

For the béchamel sauce

    2 oz (50 g) butter
    2 oz (50 g) flour
    1¼ pints (700 ml) milk
    1 teaspoon (1 × 5 ml spoon) mustard powder
    grated nutmeg
    salt and pepper
    4 oz (100–125 g) Cheddar cheese, grated

Other ingredients

    16–20 cannelloni tubes (approx.)
    ¼ pint (150 ml) single cream
    2 oz (50 g) Cheddar cheese
    8 oz (225 g) chopped watercress (optional)

* If you have a food processor, use leaf or chopped spinach. If not, use creamed or chopped spinach.

Stew the onions and the garlic in the oil and butter in a covered pan over a low heat for 20 minutes, removing the lid and stirring vigorously every few minutes.

If the spinach is chopped or whole leaf, force out any excess water through a sieve. Remove the onion from the heat, and mix in the spinach. At this point, if you have a food processor and are using whole leaf or chopped spinach, put the onion and spinach mixture into the processor for a couple of minutes until it is finely chopped but not creamed. (You may need to do this in batches.)

Beat the eggs, cream, flour, salt, pepper, nutmeg and lemon rind together in a bowl. Combine this mixture and the Parmesan and cottage cheese with the spinach and onion mixture.

Make the béchamel sauce with the ingredients stated, following the instructions on page 144. Add the 4 oz (100–125 g) grated cheese at the last minute.

Precook the cannelloni for a few minutes in salted, boiling water (see pages 4–5). I *know* manufacturers recommend using it uncooked, but in my experience there is a real danger the pasta will not absorb enough liquid and will arrive at the table still glutinous.

Stuff the cannelloni with the spinach mixture, and lay the pieces in an ovenproof dish, spreading any remaining filling on top. Add the chopped watercress to the béchamel sauce and pour over the whole dish. Cover tightly with foil and cook in a medium oven (375°F/190°C/gas mark 5) for about an hour, removing the foil after the first 45 minutes. If the dish is not sufficiently browned on top, place under a hot grill for another few minutes before serving.

Pancakes with spinach and cottage cheese, baked with tomato sauce

These pancakes ('crespolini') provide a light, delicious but sustaining alternative to lasagne or cannelloni. Serve as a starter, or with a mixed salad as a main meal.

The quantities I have given should be sufficient for about ten filled pancakes. I have been deliberately over-generous with the pancake batter as there is nothing more annoying than running out of mixture before you have made your target number of pancakes.

(You could use curd cheese instead of cottage cheese, or half quantities of each – or you could use ricotta cheese.)

For 10 generous starter or small main course helpings, use:

For the pancake batter

> 8 oz (225 g) plain flour
> 1 teaspoon (1 × 5 ml spoon) salt
> 3 eggs
> 1 egg yolk
> 1 pint (575 ml) milk
> oil for frying

For the filling

> 1½ lbs (675 g) frozen chopped spinach, *or* 2 lbs (900–925 g) fresh spinach
> a little butter
> 1 lb (450 g) cottage cheese
> salt and pepper
> grated nutmeg
> 4 oz (100–125 g) hard cheese (e.g. Gruyère), *or* 6 oz (175 g) Mozzarella

For the tomato sauce

>2 × 14 oz (2 × 400 g) tins Italian plum tomatoes
>2 teaspoons (2 × 5 ml spoons) dried oregano
>salt and pepper
>3 oz (75–100 g) grated Parmesan or Cheddar cheese

First make the pancake batter. Sift the flour and salt into a bowl. Stir in the beaten eggs and add the milk a little at a time, beating with an egg whisk to remove the lumps. If you have a food processor, you can simply process all the batter ingredients together for a couple of minutes. Leave the batter to stand for 30 minutes.

Next make the filling. Defrost the spinach, cooking for a few minutes in a little butter in a covered saucepan. If you are using fresh spinach, cook it in a very little water in a covered pan until softened, drain well, then chop it coarsely and toss in a little melted butter. Stir in the cottage cheese and season to taste, adding a little grated nutmeg at the same time.

Make the sauce by coarsely chopping the tinned tomatoes (or squeezing them through your fingers) into a bowl, and stirring in the oregano and seasoning.

Use a medium to large heavy frying pan to fry the pancakes. Heat the pan well and spread about 1 teaspoon (1 × 5 ml spoon) oil over the base with a scrap of kitchen roll. Pour in about 2 tablespoons (2 × 15 ml spoons) of pancake batter – just enough to thinly coat the bottom of the pan. Ease around the edges with a fish slice or spatula, and flip the pancake over when its base is golden brown. Cook the second side until lightly browned, then remove from the pan and stack on a plate.

Fill each pancake by laying a narrow slice of hard cheese down the centre, then a couple of spoonfuls of spinach filling spread about an inch wide down the middle of the pancake. Fold the two sides over the filling to make a roll, and then place the pancake rolls side by side in an ovenproof dish. Pour over the sauce, and sprinkle with the grated cheese. Bake in a medium oven (375°F/190°C/gas mark 5) for 30 minutes, or until the cheese has melted and slightly browned and the pancakes are heated through.

Pancakes with spinach and cottage cheese, baked with a béchamel sauce

(You can use curd cheese instead of cottage cheese.)

For 10 generous starter or small main course helpings, use:

For the pancake batter and filling

See previous recipe (page 31)

For the béchamel sauce

    1½ oz (25–50 g) butter
    1½ oz (25–50 g) plain flour
    1 pint (575 ml) milk

Other ingredients

    3 oz (75–100 g) grated Parmesan, Gruyère or Cheddar cheese

Make the béchamel sauce as instructed on page 144 (either version). Make and fill the pancakes (see page 32). Pour over them the béchamel sauce, sprinkle with the grated cheese and bake in a medium oven as in the previous recipe.

Spaghetti with courgettes and Mozzarella cheese

This makes a light but satisfying lunch or supper dish which is economical (when courgettes are in season) and easy to prepare.

(If you are unable to obtain Italian Mozzarella, or for a change, you could try Danish Mozzarella, Gruyère, Emmenthal, Leicester, Cheddar, or even a blue cheese.)

For 2 main course helpings, use:

>1 tablespoon (1 × 15 ml spoon) olive oil
>1 clove garlic, crushed
>8 oz (225 g) courgettes, finely sliced
>salt and pepper
>4 tablespoons (4 × 15 ml spoons) chicken stock (or hot water)
>8 oz (225 g) spaghetti (or tagliatelle)
>$\frac{1}{2}$ oz (15 g) butter
>a few leaves fresh basil, chopped (optional)
>*2$\frac{1}{2}$ oz (75 g) Italian Mozzarella cheese, cubed

Heat the oil in a frying pan, add the garlic and sauté for a moment before adding the courgettes. Sauté the courgettes for about 5 minutes, turning frequently, until they have started to turn golden but are still quite crisp. Add the chicken stock and seasoning, and cook for a further 3–4 minutes.

Meanwhile, cook the pasta in plenty of salted, boiling water, drain and put back into the pan. Add the butter and stir until it has melted. Stir in the vegetables, cheese and fresh herbs, and keep stirring over a low heat for a couple of minutes until the cheese has melted.

Serve immediately.

* If the cheese has become a little hard around the edges, grate it rather than cube it to give it a better chance of melting.

Spaghetti with tomatoes, red pepper, olives and Mozzarella cheese

The roast red pepper gives this dish a pleasant tangy flavour which contrasts well with the mildness and chewy quality of the cheese. Served with a green salad this makes an excellent supper dish. It looks fresh and pretty but is also substantial, and it is good enough to serve even on a special occasion.

For 2 main course helpings, use:

    1 red pepper (medium size)
    2 tablespoons (2 × 15 ml spoons) olive oil
    salt and pepper
    3 oz (75–100 g) onion, finely sliced
    8 olives (green or black), pitted and chopped
    ½ wine glass (2 fl oz/50 ml) red or white wine
    6 oz (175 g) tomatoes, skinned and coarsely chopped
    ½ teaspoon (1 × 2.5 ml spoon) dried thyme
    8 oz (225 g) spaghetti
    ½ oz (15 g) butter
    2 oz (50 g) Mozzarella cheese (or another mild, hard
        cheese), cut into small pieces

Place the whole red pepper on the grill pan, with the pepper nearly touching the heating element, and grill under a high heat. (Most of the skin will turn black but will peel off to reveal an unburnt, delicious pepper underneath.) Remove from the grill, cool slightly and peel, then cut the peeled pepper into strips and lay on a plate. Dribble ½ tablespoon (½ × 15 ml spoon) of the olive oil over the strips, and sprinkle with a little salt and pepper. Leave for a few minutes, then slice into smaller pieces.

Sauté the onion in the remaining olive oil for a few minutes until softened and translucent. Add the chopped olives and the grilled red pepper. Stir in the wine, tomatoes and the thyme. Simmer on a low heat with the lid on for 7–8 minutes, stirring occasionally and adding a little water (from the pasta pot) if the sauce is getting at all dry or is sticking to the bottom of the pan. Season.

Meanwhile, cook the pasta in plenty of salted, boiling water until 'al dente'. Drain and put back into the pan over a low heat. Stir in the butter, the sauce and the Mozzarella cheese.

Serve immediately the cheese starts to melt.

Spaghetti with aubergine, cream cheese and herbs

For 2 main course helpings, use:

3 oz (75–100 g) aubergine
½ oz (15 g) butter
1 tablespoon (1 × 15 ml spoon) olive oil
1 clove garlic, crushed
4 tablespoons (4 × 15 ml spoons) each white wine and
    chicken stock, *or* 8 tablespoons (8 × 15 ml spoons)
    chicken stock
2 tablespoons (2 × 15 ml spoons) cream (or milk)
2 oz (50 g) cream cheese
2 pinches chilli powder
½ teaspoon (1 × 2.5 ml spoon) dried thyme
salt and pepper
8 oz (225 g) spaghetti
grated Parmesan cheese (or substitute Cheddar)

First prepare the aubergine. Slice into pieces about ¼–½ inch (0.5–1 cm) thick. Spread out on a piece of kitchen roll or clean tea towel, sprinkle with salt and leave to sweat. After 10 minutes, turn the pieces over and leave to sweat from the other side.

Melt the butter over a medium heat, add the oil and stir in the crushed garlic. Add the aubergine almost immediately and sauté until it begins to look dry. At this point pour in the wine and chicken stock and simmer gently for a few minutes. (If at any point the sauce begins to look dry, add some water from the pasta pot.) Stir in the cream and the cream cheese. When the cheese has melted, stir in the chilli powder and thyme. Season.

Meanwhile, cook the pasta in plenty of salted, boiling water until 'al dente'. Drain and put back in the pan, then stir in the sauce, mixing it well with the pasta.

Serve piping hot with grated cheese on the side.

Wholewheat twists with Boursin cheese

A delicious dish that is extremely quick and easy to prepare.

For 3 main course helpings, use:

> 1 × 7½ oz (200 g) Boursin cheese with chives and garlic
> ½ oz (15 g) butter
> 4 tablespoons (4 × 15 ml spoons) single cream
> salt and pepper
> 12 oz (325–350 g) wholewheat twists

Crumble the Boursin into a bowl and put aside. Melt the butter in a pan, add the cream and seasoning, and keep warm on a very low heat.

Meanwhile, cook the pasta in plenty of salted, boiling water. Drain when 'al dente' and return to the pan on a very low heat. Pour on the warm, melted butter and cream, stir in the Boursin cheese, and continue cooking until the cheese melts and coats the pasta.

Serve immediately.

Spaghetti with mushrooms, garlic, onion, herbs and cheese

This is a simple, easy-to-cook lunch or supper dish.

For 2 main course helpings, use:

1 tablespoon (1 × 15 ml spoon) olive oil
½ oz (15 g) butter
1 clove garlic, crushed
3 oz (75–100 g) onion, finely sliced
6 oz (175 g) mushrooms, finely sliced
mixed fresh herbs (e.g. 1 tablespoon/1 × 15 ml spoon
    freshly chopped parsley, basil or coriander leaves)
1 teaspoon (1 × 5 ml spoon) dried rubbed sage, oregano or
    thyme
salt and pepper
2 tablespoons (2 × 15 ml spoons) white wine (or chicken
    stock – or hot water)
7–8 oz (200–225 g) spaghetti (or spaghettini)
3 tablespoons (3 × 15 ml spoons) fresh Parmesan, grated (or
    substitute another hard cheese)

Sauté the onion and garlic gently in the oil and butter. Add the
mushrooms, then the herbs and seasoning, and continue to
sauté for a few minutes until the mushrooms have softened and
darkened. Add the white wine and stew for a few more
minutes.

Meanwhile, cook the pasta in plenty of salted, boiling water
until 'al dente'. Drain and put back into the pan or into a
preheated serving dish. Mix in the sauce and the grated
Parmesan.

Serve immediately.

Semolina and cheese gnocchi

For 8 starter or 4 main course helpings, use:

2 pints (1150 ml) milk
grated nutmeg (to taste)
salt and pepper
8–10 oz (225–275 g) semolina
2 eggs
2 egg yolks
4 oz (100–125 g) grated Parmesan cheese
3 oz (75–100 g) grated Cheddar cheese
1½ oz (25–50 g) butter

Add the nutmeg and seasoning to the milk and bring to the boil.
Leaving the pan on a very low heat, sprinkle in the semolina, a
very little at a time, stirring constantly with a wooden spoon.
Take care not to add too much semolina at a time or lumps will
form. (If you do get lumps, beat them out with an egg whisk, or
fish them out of the pan and break them up with a fork.)
Eventually the mixture will be thick enough to stand the spoon
up in it. At this point, stop adding the semolina – even if you
still have some left – and remove the pan from the heat. Allow
to cool a little, and then stir in the eggs and egg yolks, followed
by 3 oz (75–100 g) of the grated Parmesan and all the grated
Cheddar.

Find a flat surface (you could use a kitchen table or sideboard,
or baking trays) where the gnocchi can lie undisturbed for a few
hours, or even overnight. Spread out a large piece of foil, oil it,
and spread the gnocchi mixture over it about ½ inch (1 cm) thick.
Leave for several hours, and then cut out little rounds using a
pastry cutter or tumbler, just as if you were making biscuits.
Grease a shallow ovenproof dish and spread the rounds across
the bottom so that they overlap like a spread deck of cards. Melt
the butter, pour over the gnocchi, and sprinkle the remaining
Parmesan cheese on top. Bake in a medium oven
(375°F/190°C/gas mark 4) for 20–30 minutes until well browned
on top. (If necessary, brown for a few minutes under a hot grill.)
Serve very hot.

Spaghetti with cream and cheese

This dish, although *so* simple, is quite delicious. It is much better if you can make it with fresh Parmesan.

(You can also make the dish using 4 tablespoons [4 × 15 ml spoons] Parmesan with 2 oz [50 g] skinned and chopped Brie, Camembert or other strongly flavoured soft cheese. If you have no Parmesan, Emmenthal, Gruyère or Brie are good alternatives – and you can get excellent results using an egg noodle instead of spaghetti.)

For 2 main course helpings, use:

¼ pint (150 ml) single cream
1 egg yolk
5 tablespoons (5 × 15 ml spoons) freshly grated Parmesan
salt and freshly ground black pepper
8 oz (225 g) spaghetti

Beat together the cream and egg yolk, and then stir in the cheese.

Cook the pasta in plenty of salted, boiling water until 'al dente'. Drain, and return to the pan. Pour on the sauce and cook over a low heat, stirring continuously, until the sauce thickens.

Serve immediately with freshly ground black pepper.

Wholewheat pasta with rosemary, cream and Parmesan cheese

This recipe was given to me by a great friend, Giocunda Ciconnia. Mexican by birth, she has lived for much of her life in Italy, and was married at one time to a Venetian. She and her sons are wonderful cooks. I aspire to her relaxed way of entertaining, throwing together a party at an hour's notice, serving her friends steaming bowls of pasta, in a kitchen which is also a heavenly dining room with rust-coloured lacquered walls and an open fireplace.

I find this delicately flavoured cream goes particularly well with the nutty quality of wholewheat pasta.

For 4 main course helpings, use:

> 1½ oz (25–50 g) butter
> 1 tablespoon (1 × 15 ml spoon) dried or fresh rosemary *or* 1 teaspoon (1 × 5 ml spoon) dried ground rosemary
> 1 chicken stock cube
> ½ pint (275 ml) single cream
> salt and pepper
> 1 lb (450 g) wholewheat twists, quills or tagliatelle
> 2 oz (50 g) freshly grated Parmesan cheese
> Additional Parmesan cheese to serve on the side

Melt the butter over a low heat. Add the rosemary, taking care not to let it burn. Crumble in the chicken stock cube and stir until it has dissolved. Add the cream and seasoning, and continue stirring over a very low heat for a couple of minutes.

Meanwhile, cook the pasta in plenty of salted, boiling water until 'al dente'. Drain, and put back into the pan. Add the Parmesan cheese to the sauce at the last minute before pouring it over the pasta (through a strainer if whole rosemary has been used). Stir the sauce in well. Serve very hot with additional grated Parmesan on the side.

Quills with Stilton, sage and cream

This is an excellent recipe for using up tired, leftover bits of Stilton, especially if you have indulged in a whole or half Stilton over Christmas. (You could mix in some other leftover cheese to make up the quantity if necessary.) It is also possible to substitute another strong, blue-veined cheese for the Stilton, such as Gorgonzola, Dolcelatte or Roquefort.

I like to serve this dish with a green vegetable or mixed salad, as its colour is a little bland. For the same reason you could consider using one of the coloured pastas.

For 4 main course helpings, use:

>1 oz (25 g) butter
>8 leaves fresh sage, *or* ½ teaspoon (1 × 2.5 ml spoon) dried
>   sage
>6 oz (175 g) Stilton, grated or crumbled
>¼ pint (150 ml) single cream
>salt and pepper
>1 lb (450 g) quills
>grated fresh Parmesan (optional)

Melt the butter. Add the sage and cook over a very low heat for a minute. Stir in the cheese, cream and seasoning, and continue cooking until the cheese has melted.

Meanwhile, cook the pasta in plenty of salted, boiling water until 'al dente'. Drain, put back into the pot, and mix in the sauce.

Serve immediately, with extra cheese on the side if you like.

Tagliatelle with dried and fresh mushrooms and cream

Dried mushrooms can be found in little tin-foil or Cellophane packets in good delicatessens and some supermarkets. Although they *are* expensive, you will only need one small packet for this recipe. They have an interesting, rich, slightly sweet flavour which combines well with cream. I find the sauce goes particularly well with an egg pasta such as tagliatelle, and I sometimes make this dish with (bought) fresh pasta.

For 6 starter size helpings, use:

½ oz (15 g) dried mushrooms
1½ oz (25–50 g) butter
1 clove garlic, crushed
2 oz (50 g) onion, finely chopped
12 oz (325–350 g) fresh mushrooms, finely sliced
¼ pint (5 fl oz/150 ml) double cream
10–12 oz (275–350 g) tagliatelle
grated cheese (optional)
salt and pepper

Soak the dried mushrooms in ¾ pint (15 fl oz/425 ml) warm water for 20–30 minutes until softened. Strain, reserving some of the liquid, and pat dry with kitchen paper. Then chop into small pieces.

Sauté the garlic and onion in the butter until the onion begins to soften, then add the porcini and continue to sauté for a few minutes on a low heat, taking care not to let the ingredients burn. Add 3 tablespoons (3 × 15 ml spoons) of the reserved porcini liquid, then stir in the fresh mushrooms. Place the lid on the pan and turn up the heat to allow the mushrooms to produce their juices. After a couple of minutes, stir with a wooden spoon and then continue cooking until the mushrooms are well softened. Pour in the cream, and heat through, seasoning to taste. The sauce should be reheated just before adding to the cooked pasta.

44

Cook the pasta in plenty of salted, boiling water. Drain when 'al dente' and put into a preheated serving dish or back into the pan. Stir in a knob of butter with a wooden spoon and then pour the sauce over the pasta.

Serve with grated cheese on the side if desired, though personally I prefer it without.

Tagliatelle with cream, peas, cheese and roast red pepper

This dish was invented on the spur of the moment as a celebration when a friend arrived for dinner saying he had been shopping that afternoon and had bought a house! As it was rather an exceptional house (in the 1830s the ground floor had been a tobacconist's shop at which the historian Thomas Carlyle had bought his cigars) something had to be done to spruce up the rather simple, traditional 'fresh tagliatelle with cream, peas and cheese' I had been planning. We found that the addition of a roast red pepper did the trick, adding colour and an appropriately exotic, slightly smoky flavour.

For 2 main course helpings, use:

> 1 medium red pepper
> ½ tablespoon (½ × 15 ml spoon) olive oil
> ¼ pint (150 ml) single cream
> 4 oz (100–125 g) frozen peas
> grated nutmeg (to taste)
> salt and pepper
> 9 oz (250 g) fresh tagliatelle, (or use a dried egg pasta)
> ½ oz (15 g) butter
> 2 oz (50 g) Gruyère, grated, *or* 1 oz (25 g) freshly grated
>   Parmesan

Place the whole red pepper on the grill pan with the pepper almost touching the heating element, and grill it on a high heat. (Most of the skin will turn black, but don't lose your nerve! The black skin will peel off to reveal an unburnt, slightly cooked pepper underneath.) Remove from the grill, cool slightly, and then peel off the black skin. Cut the pepper into strips about 1 inch (2.5 cm) wide. Lay the pieces on a plate and dribble the olive oil over them. Sprinkle on a little salt and pepper.

Put the cream in a pan over a low heat. When the cream is hot (*not* boiling), throw in the frozen peas, grated nutmeg and seasoning and cook for a couple of minutes, taking care not to let the cream boil. Add the pepper strips, and allow to heat through before removing the pan from the heat.

Meanwhile, cook the pasta in plenty of salted, boiling water. Drain, and put back into the pan with the butter. When the butter has melted, add the sauce and the grated cheese, stirring until the cheese has melted.

Serve immediately.

Tagliatelle with broccoli, ginger, cream and peas

For 6 starter or 3–4 main course helpings, use:

2 tablespoons (2 × 15 ml spoons) sunflower or olive oil
2 teaspoons (2 × 5 ml spoons) fresh ginger, peeled and
    finely chopped
pinch salt
6 oz (175 g) broccoli, quite finely chopped
4 oz (100–125 g) frozen peas (straight from the freezer)
¼ pint (150 ml) single or double cream
4 oz (100–125 g) cottage cheese
salt and pepper
12 oz (325–350 g) tagliatelle
grated Parmesan cheese (or substitute Emmenthal or
    Cheddar)

Heat the oil in a large frying pan or wok. Throw in the ginger
and a pinch of salt, and sauté over a medium heat for a minute
taking care not to let it burn. Add the broccoli and sauté for
another couple of minutes, turning with a wooden spoon. Next
add the frozen peas and cook for a further 2 minutes or so.
Finally, pour in the cream and cook gently for 3–4 more
minutes. Stir in the seasoning and the cottage cheese.

Meanwhile, cook the pasta in plenty of salted, boiling water
until 'al dente'. Drain and put back into the pan. Add the sauce
and cook for another minute until the pasta and sauce are
thoroughly heated through and well integrated.

Serve immediately with grated cheese on the side.

Penne Harford – quills with vodka, sage, cream and peas

This dish should really be called 'Penne Storraro', as I first came across vodka and sage sauce at a dinner given by the great film cameraman, Vittorio Storraro, while he was living in London working on the film *Reds*. However, successful experimentation over a weekend spent with some particularly enthusiastic and appreciative friends, Camilla and Gerald Harford, has caused me to rename the dish in their honour.

I add the vodka at the end of the cooking, since alcohol has a considerably lower boiling point than the other liquids, and will tend to evaporate as soon as the sauce boils. If you wish to remove the alcoholic content of the recipe, add the vodka earlier in the cooking.

For 8 starter size helpings, use:

    2 oz (50 g) butter
    12–24 sage leaves, pulled into pieces, *or* ½ teaspoon (1 × 2.5
        ml spoon) dried sage
    ½ pint (275 ml) double cream
    ¼ pint (150 ml) single cream
    8 oz (225 g) frozen peas (straight from the freezer)
    9 tablespoons (9 × 15 ml spoons) vodka
    salt and pepper
    1 oz (25 g) freshly grated Parmesan (plus additional
        Parmesan on the side)
    1 lb (450 g) quills (penne)

Melt the butter in a pan. Add the sage and leave on a very low heat for a couple of minutes to allow the herb flavour to infuse the butter. Pour in both the double and single cream and stir well. Throw in the frozen peas and continue cooking for another few minutes until the peas are barely done and still have a bite. Add the vodka and seasoning, and remove the pan from the heat until the pasta is ready. The Parmesan cheese should be added to the sauce at the last minute before mixing with the pasta.

Meanwhile, cook the pasta in plenty of salted, boiling water until 'al dente'. Drain and return to the pan. Pour the sauce over the pasta and continue cooking for a minute or two, stirring with a wooden spoon.

Serve very hot with additional grated Parmesan cheese on the side.

Quills with vodka, tomato and cream

I find pasta tubes of one sort or another particularly suitable for this recipe as they have a way of retaining the sauce most successfully, making a very succulent dish. I would recommend quills for all the vodka sauces, but you could use any other short tube pasta.

I have a rule of thumb for the quantity of vodka in these recipes, reminiscent of a certain tea advertiser in the sixties and seventies – one spoon of vodka per person and one for the pot!

For 8 starter size helpings, use:

> 2 oz (50 g) butter
> 6 tablespoons (6 × 15 ml spoons) tomato purée
> ¾ pint (425 ml) single cream
> 9 tablespoons (9 × 15 ml spoons) vodka
> salt and pepper
> 1 lb (450 g) quills

Melt the butter over a low heat. Stir in the tomato purée and the cream. Remove from the heat and add the vodka and seasoning.

Meanwhile, cook the pasta in plenty of salted, boiling water until 'al dente'. Drain, and put back into the pan or into a preheated serving dish. Reheat the sauce if necessary, taking care not to let it boil, and mix into the pasta.

Serve immediately.

Note: If you want to burn off the alcohol content, add the vodka to the butter, mix in the tomato purée, and allow to bubble for a few minutes.

The following recipes in this section include no animal products – cheese on the side, where suggested, is of course optional.

Spaghetti with oil and garlic

Spaghetti with oil – or butter – and garlic is delicious (if you like garlic), especially if you use good quality olive oil and fresh garlic. Since garlic is extremely good for the digestion and for chasing away the common cold, this dish is also therapeutic.

The olive oil version is known in Italy as 'Spaghetti con aglio e olio'. Serve it with a big, juicy mixed salad.

For 2 main course helpings, use:

> 3 tablespoons (3 × 15 ml spoons) olive oil, *or* 2 oz (50 g)
>   butter
> *1–3 cloves garlic (according to taste and the size of the
>   cloves), crushed
> salt and freshly ground black pepper (preferably sea salt)
> 8 oz (225 g) spaghetti

Sauté the garlic in the oil *very gently* on a low heat for a couple of minutes. If allowed to get too hot, the garlic will burn and become bitter, turning deep gold or brown. If this happens, strain off the garlic pieces and begin again, using the same oil but fresh garlic. (Italian purists don't even attempt to cook the garlic – they just put raw garlic straight on to the pasta with the oil!)

Meanwhile, cook the pasta in plenty of salted, boiling water until 'al dente'. Drain and put back into the pan. Pour over the oil and garlic, season with salt and pepper, and continue cooking for a minute or so, stirring well.

* If you find this amount of garlic more than you can take, leave the cloves whole and remove them from the oil just before pouring it over the pasta.

Spaghetti with oil, garlic and herbs

This dish, made with the maximum amount of garlic (raw, of course!) and parsley, is the Italian version of the quick sandwich or toasted cheese snack . . .

For 2 main course helpings:

Proceed as for 'Spaghetti with oil and garlic' (page 52) adding:

> 1–2 tablespoons (1–2 × 15 ml spoons) fresh chopped herbs (parsley, basil or coriander) *or* $\frac{1}{2}$ tablespoon ($\frac{1}{2}$ × 15 ml spoon) dried herbs

The herbs should be added to the oil (or butter) just before it is mixed into the pasta.

Spaghetti with oil, garlic and chilli

In Italy this is traditionally the dish that men prepare for their friends after a long night on the tiles. Whether this is because they do not dare wake their wives at such a late hour and in a drunken state, or whether it is because the dish has therapeutic properties against a hangover, I don't know! Whatever the reason, it is an excellent storecupboard standby for a quick supper, good for late on a Sunday night to eat in front of the telly.

For 2 main course helpings, use:

>   3 tablespoons (3 × 15 ml spoons) olive oil
>   1–3 cloves garlic (according to taste), crushed
>   *1–2 dried red chillis, chopped, or ½–1 teaspoon (½–1 × 5 ml spoon) chilli powder
>   salt and pepper
>   8 oz (225 g) spaghetti (or quills or bows)
>   grated Parmesan or Cheddar cheese (optional)

Sauté the garlic and the chilli in the oil over a *very gentle* heat (see comments on 'Spaghetti with oil and garlic', page 52). Add salt and pepper to taste.

Meanwhile, cook the pasta in plenty of salted, boiling water until 'al dente'. Drain and put back into the pan. Pour the oil, garlic and chilli over the pasta and stir in well.

Serve very hot with grated cheese on the side if you like.

* The amount of chilli used in this recipe is entirely according to taste: if you like very hot food then, obviously, use a lot of chilli. But don't forget, while tasting the sauce, that the blandness of the pasta will dilute the power of the chilli quite considerably.

Spaghetti with spruced-up bottled pesto sauce

Unless you grow your own basil in large quantities it is hardly practical to make fresh pesto sauce. If, however, you *do* have a massive basil crop, it is worth considering making your own basil sauce and then freezing it for use later in the year.

It is possible to buy bottled pesto sauce in good Italian delicatessens. Brands vary in quality. I have tried Tigullio which I find quite excellent when spruced up a bit with good olive oil and garlic. These bottled sauces have the added advantage of being comparatively inexpensive, considering the price of fresh basil and pine nuts.

For 4 main course helpings, use:

>4 tablespoons (4 × 15 ml spoons) bottled pesto sauce
>4 tablespoons (4 × 15 ml spoons) good olive oil
>2 cloves garlic, crushed
>4 tablespoons (4 × 15 ml spoons) hot water
>salt and pepper
>1 lb (450 g) spaghetti (or spaghettini)
>2 tablespoons (2 × 15 ml spoons) freshly grated Parmesan
>   cheese

In a small bowl, mix the pesto sauce with the oil, garlic and hot water.

Meanwhile, cook the pasta in plenty of salted, boiling water. Drain and put into a preheated serving dish. Spoon on the pesto sauce, sprinkle on Parmesan cheese, and mix together well.

Serve immediately with freshly ground black pepper on each helping.

Spaghetti with bottled pesto sauce and mushrooms

For 4 main course helpings, use:

5 tablespoons (5 × 15 ml spoons) good olive oil
8 oz (225 g) mushrooms, sliced
2–4 cloves garlic, crushed
4 tablespoons (4 × 15 ml spoons) hot water (from the pasta pot)
4 tablespoons (4 × 15 ml spoons) bottled pesto sauce
1 lb (450 g) spaghetti
grated Parmesan cheese on the side

Sauté the mushrooms in 4 tablespoons (4 × 15 ml spoons) of the oil until they soften and slightly darken. Mix together the crushed garlic, hot water and pesto sauce in a cup. Add to the mushrooms and stir well with a wooden spoon.

Meanwhile, cook the pasta in plenty of salted, boiling water until 'al dente'. Drain and return to the pan (or put into a preheated serving dish). Stir in the remaining olive oil, the mushrooms and pesto sauce.

Serve immediately, with Parmesan on the side.

Spaghetti with traditional tomato sauce

One of the most delicious pasta dishes I have ever eaten was pasta served with a simple tomato sauce. I was on the Greek island of Patmos, and I suppose it was the quality of the ingredients – fresh plum tomatoes, local olive oil and freshly picked herbs from the mountainside – which made such a simple sauce *so* exquisite. This is, of course, of little consolation to the English cook struggling with locally available ingredients. Nevertheless, an English version of the classic Italian tomato sauce is also delicious when carefully prepared and gently stewed for an adequate length of time.

If you cannot find any tasty fresh tomatoes, use tinned Italian plum tomatoes (see page 10).

For 2 main course helpings, use:

> 3 tablespoons (3 × 15 ml spoons) olive oil
> 4 oz (100–125 g) onion, chopped
> 2 cloves garlic, crushed
> 1 lb (450 g) fresh tomatoes, skinned and coarsely chopped,
>   *or* 14 oz (400 g) tinned Italian plum tomatoes
> 1 teaspoon (1 × 5 ml spoon) sugar (optional)
> herbs to taste (e.g. 2 teaspoons/2 × 5 ml spoons dried
>   oregano)
> salt and pepper
> 8 oz (225 g) spaghetti
> freshly grated Parmesan cheese

Sauté the onion and garlic in the oil over a low heat for several minutes until the onion is translucent. Add the tomatoes, sugar, herbs and seasoning. (If you are using tinned tomatoes break them up in the pan with a wooden spoon.) Simmer in a covered pan for 20–25 minutes, stirring frequently.

Meanwhile, cook the pasta in plenty of salted boiling water until 'al dente'. Drain, and put back into the pan or into a preheated serving dish. Add the sauce and mix together well.

Serve with grated cheese on the side.

VARIATIONS

For a change, throw in a few black olives, stoned and halved. Add them to the oil while the onion is softening.

For a spicier version, add half a small dried red chilli, seeded and chopped, again while the onion is softening. There is a famous Italian dish, 'Penne all'arrabbiata' (literally, 'Angry quills'!) which consists of quills in a hot tomato sauce.

Another variation would be to add some chopped fried bacon (about 2 oz/50 g) to the sautéd onions.

Spaghetti with quick, spicy tomato sauce

For 2 main course helpings, use:

2 tablespoons (2 × 15 ml spoons) olive oil
4 oz (100–125 g) onion, finely sliced
¼ teaspoon (½ × 2.5 ml spoon) chilli powder
14 oz (400 g) fresh tomatoes, skinned *or* tinned tomatoes
2 cloves garlic, crushed
8 oz (225 g) spaghetti (or pasta shapes)
grated Parmesan cheese on the side

Sauté the onion in the oil until softened and translucent.
Sprinkle in the chilli powder and stir well. Add the tomatoes
and, if they are fresh rather than tinned, add an extra 2
tablespoons (2 × 15 ml spoons) hot water. Stew for a few
minutes, then add the garlic and continue to cook until the pasta
is ready. If you feel the sauce needs it, add more chilli, a very
little at a time.

Cook the pasta in plenty of salted, boiling water until 'al
dente'. Drain, return either to the pan or to a preheated serving
dish, and mix in the sauce.

Serve with grated cheese on the side.

Quills with quick and simple tomato sauce

One of the disadvantages of tomato sauce is that, unless the recipe uses fresh tomatoes, the sauce – however simple – takes so long to cook. Here is an absolutely delicious, quick version that you can make while the pasta is cooking.

For 4 main course helpings, use:

> 4 tablespoons (4 × 15 ml spoons) olive oil
> 1–2 cloves garlic, crushed
> 6 tablespoons (6 × 15 ml spoons) tomato purée
> 2 teaspoons (2 × 5 ml spoons) dried herbs
> ½ pint (275 ml) chicken stock (made with 1 stock cube and
>   hot water)
> 1 teaspoon (1 × 5 ml spoon) sugar
> salt and pepper
> 13 oz (375 g) quills
> grated Parmesan

Pour the oil into a large saucepan over a low to medium heat. Add the garlic, and almost immediately stir in the tomato purée. Continue stirring until the purée is well integrated with the oil, and then add the herbs and chicken stock, a little at a time. When the sauce is smooth, add the sugar and the seasoning and leave to simmer on a low heat for a few minutes.

Meanwhile, cook the pasta in plenty of salted, boiling water until 'al dente'. Drain and put into the pan containing the sauce. Continue cooking the pasta and the sauce for a couple of minutes, turning with a wooden spoon.

Serve immediately with grated cheese on the side.

Macaroni with tomato and orange

This dish is very light and fresh, and particularly good in summer. The addition of the orange zest and juice to the tomato sauce gives it an unusual flavour.

For 4 main course helpings, use:

> 2 tablespoons (2 × 15 ml spoons) olive oil
> 6 oz (175 g) onion, finely sliced
> 1½ lb (675 g) fresh tomatoes, skinned *or* tinned tomatoes
> grated zest and juice of ½ orange
> salt and pepper
> 1 lb (450 g) macaroni
> grated Parmesan cheese (or substitute Cheddar)

Sauté the onion in the olive oil over a low heat until softened and translucent. Add the tomatoes, orange juice and zest, and salt and pepper. Simmer until the sauce has reduced by about half.

Meanwhile, cook the pasta in plenty of salted, boiling water until 'al dente'. Drain, and put back into the pan or into a preheated serving dish. Mix in the sauce.

Serve immediately with grated cheese on the side.

Loyd's very spicy butterflies with aubergine and tomato

This is one of Loyd Grossman's specials. The tomato sauce on its own is incredibly hot; you should taste only with great care – it burns! Added to the pasta and mixed with the aubergine it becomes no more than pleasantly spicy. Nevertheless, the amount of red chilli you use should be 'to taste' and not dictated by my recipe. I happen to adore spicy foods!

For 8 starter size helpings, use:

>2 medium aubergines (about 8 oz/225 g each)
>7 tablespoons (7 × 15 ml spoons) olive oil (approx.)
>4 oz (100–125 g) onion
>2 cloves garlic, crushed
>2–4 small, dried red chillies (to taste), finely chopped
>14 oz (400 g) tinned Italian tomatoes
>salt and pepper
>1 lb (450 g) butterflies (or bows)
>grated cheese (optional)

Cut the aubergines into slices about ¼ inch (0.5 cm) thick. Arrange on a generously oiled baking sheet, dribble a little more oil on top of the slices, and bake in a hot oven (400°F/200°C/gas mark 6) for about 20 minutes, turning every 5 minutes or so and adding more oil if necessary.

Sauté the onion and garlic in 2 tablespoons (2 × 15 ml spoons) oil. Add the chopped chillies, tomatoes (breaking them up with a wooden spoon), and salt and pepper. Cook for a further 15–20 minutes until the sauce thickens.

Chop the baked aubergine slices into little pieces and stir into the tomato sauce. Add about ⅛–¼ pint (75–150 ml) water (or chicken stock) – enough to make a suitable quantity of adequately liquid sauce.

Meanwhile, cook the pasta in plenty of salted boiling water. Drain, put back into the pan or into a preheated serving dish, and mix in the sauce.

Serve immediately, with grated cheese on the side if you think it needs it.

Penne primavera

This dish is an improvisation on a well-known Italian theme, pasta primavera. The ingredients came from a local supermarket where I bought whatever fresh vegetables caught my eye. The dish can be eaten hot or cold.

As with most of my pasta recipes, I recommend that you, too, improvise a little if you feel like it. You could substitute various other vegetables including fennel, mushrooms, fresh peas, cauliflower, asparagus, red pepper – and particularly courgettes.

For 4 main course helpings, use:

> 4 oz (100–125 g) broccoli, broken into small pieces
> 4 oz (100–125 g) small French beans, cut into 2 inch (5 cm) lengths
> 4 oz (100–125 g) carrots, julienned or cut into thin sticks
> 4 oz (100–125 g) mange-tout peas (if available)
> 2 tablespoons (2 × 15 ml spoons) fresh, chopped herbs *or* $\frac{1}{2}$ tablespoon ($\frac{1}{2}$ × 15 ml spoon) dried herbs
> 1 lb (450 g) quills

For the vinaigrette

> 9 tablespoons (9 × 15 ml spoons) olive oil
> 3 tablespoons (3 × 15 ml spoons) wine vinegar
> 2 teaspoons (2 × 5 ml spoons) mustard (French or German) *or* 1 teaspoon (1 × 5 ml spoon) English mustard
> 1 teaspoon (1 × 5 ml spoon) caster sugar
> freshly grated nutmeg (optional)
> 1 clove garlic, crushed (optional)
> salt and pepper

Steam the vegetables for 2–4 minutes until slightly softened but still brightly coloured and crisp. If you do not possess a steamer, then boil the vegetables one at a time for just 1–2 minutes, using a slotted spoon to remove them so that you can re-use the boiling water. Drain, and put all the vegetables into a large bowl. Beat the vinaigrette ingredients together in a cup using a fork, and pour over the vegetables. Add fresh or dried herbs. Mix well.

Meanwhile, cook the pasta in salted, boiling water until 'al dente'. Drain, and mix into the bowl of vegetables and vinaigrette.

Serve either hot or cold.

Wholewheat spaghetti with summer tomatoes

Weight watchers can safely include this dish in a calorie-
controlled diet. For the quantities given below, count about 220
calories per portion.

It is only worth making this recipe if you can get hold of some
really fresh, tasty tomatoes. The dish will not be successful if you
use one of the rather bland, dull varieties that are often all there is
to be found in the shops.

You can peel the tomatoes if you like, dipping them first in the
boiling water in which you are about to cook the pasta, but with
this recipe I find the skin perfectly acceptable.

For 2 diet portions, use:

>2 teaspoons (2 × 5 ml spoons) olive oil
>½ oz (15 g) spring onions, finely chopped
>1 clove garlic, crushed
>12 oz (325–350 g) fresh tomatoes, chopped
>a little grated orange peel
>2 tablespoons (2 × 15 ml spoons) orange juice
>1 tablespoon (1 × 15 ml spoon) chopped fresh herbs (e.g.
>   parsley, basil, chives), *or* ½ tablespoon (½ × 15 ml spoon)
>   dried herbs (e.g. oregano, basil)
>1 teaspoon (1 × 5 ml spoon) caster sugar
>salt and pepper
>3 oz (75–100 g) wholewheat spaghetti (or different pasta
>   shape)

Sauté the garlic and spring onions in the olive oil over a medium
heat for a minute, taking particular care, with such a small
amount of oil, that the ingredients do not burn. Take the pan off
the heat, stir in all the other sauce ingredients, and return it to the
stove. Cook over a medium heat until the mixture is well heated
through – this should take only a couple of minutes.

Meanwhile, cook the spaghetti in plenty of salted, boiling
water. Drain and put back into the pan. Add the sauce and turn
well with a wooden spoon to make sure the sauce is well
integrated with the pasta.

Serve very hot.

Wholewheat spaghetti with slimming tomato sauce

An individual portion of this dish provides approximately 170 calories.

For 2 diet portions, use:

> 12 oz (325–350 g) tomatoes, tinned or fresh
> salt and pepper
> 1 teaspoon (1 × 5 ml spoon) dried herbs, e.g. oregano *or* 1
>   tablespoon (1 × 15 ml spoon) fresh herbs
> 3 oz (75–100 g) wholewheat spaghetti

If you are using fresh tomatoes, skin them first by dipping them in the boiling water in which you are about to cook the pasta. Chop the tomatoes coarsely and put into a small saucepan with the seasoning and herbs. Stew gently on a low heat for about 10 minutes.

Meanwhile, cook the pasta in plenty of salted, boiling water. Drain while still 'al dente', and stir in the tomato sauce.

Serve very hot.

Wholewheat pasta shells with onions, leeks, mushrooms and tofu

'Tofu' is another name for soya bean curd. Tofu is high in protein, low in calories, and although it could be accused of having a bland flavour, it is delicious when combined with such ingredients as soy sauce and sesame seeds. You can buy it at most health food shops.

For 8 starter size helpings, use:

> 2 tablespoons (2 × 15 ml spoons) sesame seed oil *or* 1
>   tablespoon (1 × 15 ml spoon) oil plus ½ oz (15 g) butter
> 4 oz (100–125 g) onions or shallots, finely sliced
> 4 oz (100–125 g) leeks, finely sliced
> 4 oz (100–125 g) mushrooms, finely sliced
> 5 oz (150 g) tofu
> 2 tablespoons (2 × 15 ml spoons) fresh, chopped parsley
> 1 lb (450 g) wholewheat pasta shells
> soy sauce, to taste (optional)

Place the onions and leeks with the oil in a covered pan, and cook over a very low heat for 15–20 minutes, stirring occasionally, until the vegetables are soft and mushy. Add the mushrooms and cook for a further 3–4 minutes. Mix in the tofu with a wooden spoon, breaking it up until it is well blended with the other ingredients. Simmer gently for 5 more minutes. Stir in the chopped parsley at the last moment before adding the mixture to the pasta.

Meanwhile, cook the pasta in plenty of salted, boiling water. Drain when 'al dente' and put into a preheated serving dish. Stir in the sauce.

Serve very hot with soy sauce on the side.

Wholewheat spaghetti with carrots, orange juice and soy sauce

For 2 main course helpings, use:

2 tablespoons (2 × 15 ml spoons) olive oil
2 oz (50 g) onion, finely sliced
1 small clove garlic, crushed
6 oz (175 g) carrots, grated or finely chopped
3 tablespoons (3 × 15 ml spoons) orange juice
4 tablespoons (4 × 15 ml spoons) chicken stock or water
1 tablespoon (1 × 15 ml spoon) fresh, chopped parsley
salt and pepper
8 oz (225 g) wholewheat spaghetti
2 tablespoons (2 × 15 ml spoons) soy sauce (approx.)

Sauté the onion and garlic gently in the oil until softened. Add the carrots and turn for a minute in the oil. Then stir in the orange juice and chicken stock. Season to taste. At the last moment, add the chopped parsley.

Meanwhile, cook the pasta in plenty of salted, boiling water. Drain and put into a preheated serving dish and mix in the sauce. Serve immediately, with a sprinkling of soy sauce to taste on each helping.

Wholewheat spaghetti with stir-fried vegetables

Ideally you should stir-fry the vegetables in a wok. If you don't possess one, use a large, heavy frying pan or saucepan. The process of stir-frying is, in a nutshell, to sauté and turn the vegetables continuously with a wooden spoon over a high heat so that they cook quickly without burning and retain a slightly crispy texture. Slice the vegetables *before* you begin to cook and leave them ready on separate plates. The stir-frying process is so fast that you won't have time to prepare them as you go along.

Feel free to substitute other vegetables in season in whatever quantities and proportions you choose. Courgettes, turnips, cauliflower, Chinese cabbage and spinach would all be appropriate. You could even make the whole dish using just one vegetable.

For 4 main course helpings, use:

> 2 tablespoons (2 × 15 ml spoons) nut or vegetable oil
> 1 clove garlic, crushed
> pinch salt
> 1 teaspoon (1 × 5 ml spoon) fresh ginger root, finely chopped (optional)
> 8 oz (225 g) carrots, finely sliced
> 8 oz (225 g) leeks, finely sliced
> 4 oz (100–125 g) broccoli, finely sliced
> 4 oz (100–125 g) mushrooms, finely sliced
> 2 tablespoons (2 × 15 ml spoons) chicken or vegetable stock
> 1 tablespoon (1 × 15 ml spoon) soy sauce
> 1 teaspoon (1 × 5 ml spoon) sugar
> 1 lb (450 g) wholewheat spaghetti

Sauté the garlic, salt and ginger in the oil for just a minute over a fairly high heat. Turn up the heat and throw in first whichever vegetable you think will take the longest to cook. Stir-fry for a minute or so, then add the next vegetable. Continue this way until all the prepared vegetables have been added to the pan. Stir-fry all the vegetables together for another couple of minutes before adding the stock, soy sauce and sugar. Continue frying and stirring for a little longer until the vegetables are cooked but still crispy.

Meanwhile, cook the pasta in plenty of salted, boiling water until 'al dente'. Drain, and either put into the wok with the vegetables, or back into the pasta pot with the stir-fried vegetables on top. Heat through and mix together thoroughly.

Serve with grated cheese on the side.

Meat dishes

COOKING AND SERVING PASTA

Choice of pasta

You don't have to use the pasta type specified in a particular recipe, but if you want to use another type bear in mind that as a general rule it is best to substitute one pasta type with another of similar characteristics (see page 8).

Timing

The time needed for pasta to cook can vary so much that I have not specified cooking times in the recipes. Aim to have the pasta ready at the same time as the sauce, and test it frequently as it nears the 'al dente' stage (see pages 2–4).

Serve it *hot*!

Hot pasta dishes should be served while they are still *very* hot. Always preheat plates and serving dishes.

'Cheese on the side'

Not all pasta dishes are improved by adding grated cheese. Serve it as a side dish to be added only if needed – *after* tasting.

Spaghetti with meat and tomato sauce (Mark 1)

This is my variation of a sauce usually know as 'bolognese' or simply as 'ragu'. (I sometimes substitute a small piece of pork, such as a chop or a pork sausage, demolished in the Magimix [or finely chopped] for the equivalent weight of the beef.)

For 4 main course helpings, use:

1 oz (25 g) butter
4 oz (100–125 g) onion, finely sliced
1 medium carrot, finely chopped or grated
1 stick celery, finely chopped (optional)
2 oz (50 g) bacon, rinded and chopped
1 lb (450 g) minced beef
4 tablespoons (4 × 15 ml spoons) tomato purée
1 wine glass (4 fl oz/125 ml) wine
$\frac{1}{4}$ teaspoon ($\frac{1}{2}$ × 2.5 ml spoon) ground nutmeg (optional)
$\frac{1}{2}$ teaspoon (1 × 2.5 ml spoon) dried thyme (optional)
$\frac{1}{2}$ teaspoon (1 × 2.5 ml spoon) dried oregano (optional)
4 tablespoons (4 × 15 ml spoons) single cream (optional)
salt and pepper
$\frac{1}{4}$ pint (150 ml) chicken stock (or hot water)
freshly grated Parmesan (or Cheddar) cheese
1 lb (450 g) spaghetti (or tagliatelle)

Sauté the onion, carrot and celery in the butter for a few minutes until softened. Add the bacon and continue to cook for 2–3 minutes. Then add the meat, and cook – turning with a wooden spoon – until well browned. Stir in the tomato purée, wine and herbs, followed by the stock. Cover and simmer for 40 minutes, stirring occasionally. (If the sauce becomes too dry, add a little more water.) Adjust the seasoning, adding additional salt and pepper if necessary. Stir in the cream (if used) just before serving.

Meanwhile, cook the pasta in plenty of salted, boiling water until 'al dente'. Drain, put into a preheated serving dish, and pour over the sauce.

Serve with grated cheese on the side.

Spaghetti with meat and tomato sauce (Mark 2)

For 4 main course helpings, use:

2 tablespoons (2 × 15 ml spoons) olive oil
2 cloves garlic, crushed
4 oz (100–125 g) onion, finely sliced
½ tablespoon (½ × 15 ml spoon) flour
1 lb (450 g) minced beef
14 oz (400 g) tinned Italian tomatoes
1 tablespoon (1 × 15 ml spoon) tomato purée
¼ pint (150 ml) hot water (in which you can dissolve ½
   chicken stock cube)
herbs to taste (e.g. dried oregano, marjoram)
salt and pepper
1 lb (450 g) wholewheat spaghetti (or pasta tubes)
freshly grated Parmesan (or Cheddar) cheese

Sauté the onion and garlic in the oil over a low heat, taking care not to burn the garlic, until the onion is well softened (about 10 minutes). Add the flour and stir well to integrate. Next add the meat and sauté until browned. Stir in the tomatoes – breaking them up a little with a wooden spoon – the tomato purée, herbs, seasoning and the hot water or chicken stock. Simmer over a low heat with the pan covered for 40 minutes, stirring occasionally.

Meanwhile, cook the pasta in plenty of salted, boiling water until 'al dente'. Drain, put into a preheated serving dish, and pour over the sauce.

Serve piping hot with cheese on the side.

Lasagne al forno

The most commonly served lasagne in Great Britain is probably this traditional dish, incorporating a bolognese 'ragu' (meat and tomato sauce) with a béchamel sauce and the lasagne. It is delicious and very substantial, and can be cooked or prepared in advance and reheated or cooked at the last minute. It should definitely be served with something green: a crisp vegetable such as broccoli, mange-tout peas or courgettes, or with a huge salad. There are of course endless recipes and variations; this is the one I use.

(Instead of bacon you can use a small piece of pork, or a pork sausage, finely chopped or demolished in the food processor; or you could add an extra 4 oz (100–125 g) minced beef in place of bacon or pork.)

For 6–8 main course helpings, use:

For the meat filling

> 1½ oz (25–50 g) butter
> 6 oz (175 g) onion, finely sliced
> 1 medium carrot, finely chopped or grated
> 1 stick celery, finely chopped (optional)
> 4 oz (100–125 g) bacon, rinded and chopped
> 1½ lb (675 g) minced beef
> 6 tablespoons (6 × 15 ml spoons) tomato purée
> 1 glass (4 fl oz/125 ml) wine
> ½ teaspoon (1 × 2.5 ml spoon) each dried oregano and thyme (or substitute other dried herbs)
> grated nutmeg (to taste – I might use ⅛–¼ of a whole nutmeg)
> ¼ pint (150 ml) chicken stock (or hot water)
> salt and pepper
> 4 tablespoons (4 × 15 ml spoons) single cream (optional)

For the béchamel sauce

　　2½ oz (75 g) butter
　　2½ oz (75 g) flour
　　1½ pints (875 ml) milk
　　1 bay leaf
　　grated nutmeg
　　salt and pepper

Other ingredients

　　16–20 oz lasagne (450–575 g)
　　2 oz (50 g) grated Parmesan cheese (or substitute Cheddar)

Sauté the onion, celery and carrot in the butter for a few minutes until softened. Add the bacon (or pork) and continue to sauté for a couple of minutes. Add the minced beef, and cook, turning with a wooden spoon, until the meat is browned. Stir in the tomato purée, wine, herbs and nutmeg. Add the stock or hot water and simmer, covered, for 40 minutes, stirring continuously. Season. (If it appears too dry, add some extra water or stock.) Finally, stir in the cream.

Add the grated nutmeg and bay leaf to the milk in a saucepan. Bring slowly to the boil. Remove from the heat and leave to sit for 5–10 minutes. Strain. Then make the béchamel sauce following the instructions on page 144.

Cook the lasagne as instructed on pages 4–5.

Now take a large ovenproof dish. Spread a thin layer of the meat sauce on the bottom, just covering the surface. Spoon on some béchamel sauce, season, and then lay a layer of lasagne, overlapping at the edges. Repeat the layers until you have used up all the ingredients, ending with a layer of meat followed by béchamel sauce. (I usually achieve only 2 or 3 layers). Sprinkle the cheese on top and bake in a preheated oven (375°F/190°C/gas mark 5) for about an hour. Brown the top under a hot grill at the last moment if necessary.

Aubergine, tomato and meat lasagne

For this recipe you simply need to follow the instructions for Lasagne al forno on page 75, inserting an extra layer of aubergine mixture, made as follows:

For 8–10 main course helpings, use:

4 tablespoons (4 × 15 ml spoons) olive oil
1 clove garlic, crushed
6 oz (175 g) onion, finely sliced
18 oz (500–525 g) aubergine, cut into medium slices
14 oz (400 g) tinned Italian tomatoes
¼ pint (150 ml) chicken stock (fresh, or made with ¼ stock cube)
salt and pepper

Place the onion, garlic and olive oil in a small casserole and put into a very low oven (275°F/140°C/gas mark 1) for 30 minutes, stirring occasionally. Meanwhile, lay the aubergine slices on some paper kitchen roll or a clean cloth, and sprinkle with salt. After 15 minutes, turn them over, allowing the paper or cloth to absorb the 'sweat'. Cut the slices into quarters. Remove the casserole from the oven and put on a low heat on top of the stove. Add the aubergine pieces, tinned tomatoes and chicken stock, stirring well together. Simmer for about 20 minutes, stirring occasionally, and taking care not to let the contents of the pan stick to the bottom. Season to taste, and put aside.

Make meat and béchamel sauces as for Lasagne al forno (page 75). Then layer the sauces and the lasagne as described in that recipe, but adding a layer of aubergine after each layer of lasagne, until all the ingredients have been used up. (You may need to use a larger dish than for the lasagne al forno.) Bake in the oven for an hour as described on page 76.

McEvitt's bows with meat sauce

This exceptionally delicious dish was created by an American friend, Frank McEvitt, so confirming my theory that men make the most marvellous cooks once they conquer their initial fear of the kitchen.

For 4–6 main course helpings, use:

> 2 tablespoons (2 × 15 ml spoons) olive oil
> 1 oz (25 g) butter
> 6 oz (175 g) onions or shallots, finely chopped
> 1 lb (450 g) minced beef or veal
> ¼ teaspoon (½ × 2.5 ml spoon) chilli powder (to taste)
> salt and pepper
> 1½ wine glasses (6 fl oz/175 ml) white wine
> ½ pint (275 ml) double cream
> 1 oz (25 g) fresh chopped parsley
> 3 oz (75–100 g) Parmesan cheese, grated
> 18–22 oz (500–575 g) bows or other pasta shape

Melt the butter with the oil in a large, fairly deep, frying pan. Add the onions and sauté until they become translucent and begin to turn golden (about 4–5 minutes). Stir in the meat, breaking it up with a wooden spoon and taking care that it doesn't stick. When the meat is browned, stir in the chilli powder and seasoning. Then add the white wine and reduce the liquid in the pan by turning up the heat and allowing the contents of the pan to boil for a couple of minutes. Reduce the heat again, add the cream and parsley, and cook for a further 10 minutes over the low heat.

Meanwhile, cook the pasta in plenty of salted, boiling water. Drain and put into a preheated serving dish. At the last minute add the Parmesan cheese to the sauce, then pour the sauce on to the pasta, mixing it in well.

Serve with extra grated cheese on the side.

Rigatoni with spicy meat and chicken liver ragu

I invented this as an alternative to a bolognese sauce or 'ragu'. It is spicy and interesting, without being too hot. The large ribbed pasta tubes, rigatoni, seem to be particularly successful in this recipe, but you could use any pasta shape or type you like. Served with a green vegetable or mixed salad, followed by a light dessert, cheese or fruit, it makes a satisfying meal.

For 6 main course helpings, use:

> 1 oz (25 g) butter
> 3 tablespoons (3 × 15 ml spoons) olive oil
> 2 cloves garlic, chopped or crushed
> 6 oz (175 g) onion, sliced
> 4 oz (100–125 g) carrot, chopped
> 4 oz (100–125 g) smoked, streaky bacon, chopped
> *1 teaspoon (1 × 5 ml spoon) garam marsala
> *1 teaspoon (1 × 5 ml spoon) ground coriander
> *¼ teaspoon (½ × 2.5 ml spoon) chilli powder
> 8 oz (225 g) chicken livers, coarsely chopped
> 1 lb (450 g) minced beef
> 5 tablespoons (5 × 15 ml spoons) tomato purée
> 1 wine glass (4 fl oz/ 125 ml) wine (red or white)
> ½ pint (275 ml) chicken stock
> 3 bay leaves
> salt and pepper
> 2 tablespoons (2 × 15 ml spoons) cream (optional)
> 1 lb 5 oz (600 g) rigatoni (or other pasta tubes)
> Parmesan cheese, grated

Sauté the onion and garlic in the oil and butter over a low heat until translucent. Add the carrot and bacon and continue to sauté until the bacon is browned. Stir in the spices with a wooden spoon. Keep stirring: the spices absorb a lot of the oil, and it is important to prevent the mixture from sticking to the

* The quantity of spices can be adjusted according to taste.

79

bottom of the pan and burning. Add the chicken livers and sauté until browned, then add the minced beef. When the beef has browned, stir in the tomato purée, and add the wine, chicken stock, bay leaves and seasoning. Simmer in a covered pan for about 40 minutes, stirring occasionally to make sure the mixture isn't sticking and adding more liquid (chicken stock, wine or water) if it appears too dry.

Meanwhile, cook the pasta in plenty of salted, boiling water. Drain. Stir the cream (if used) into the sauce, check the seasoning, and mix immediately with the hot, cooked pasta in a preheated serving dish.

Serve with grated Parmesan cheese on the side.

Stir-fried steak and tagliatelle

This dish is an excellent way of turning a planned grilled steak dinner for two into an impromptu supper for four. You could use pork or lamb (chops for example) instead of steak.

For 4 main course helpings, use:

2 tablespoons (2 × 15 ml spoons) vegetable oil
1 clove garlic, crushed
1 teaspoon (1 × 5 ml spoon) fresh ginger, finely chopped
1 oz (25 g) onion, finely chopped
salt (preferably sea salt) and pepper
6–8 oz (175–225 g) steak, cut into very thin 1½ inch (3.5 cm) strips
6 oz (175 g) Brussels sprouts, (or another vegetable) finely sliced
4 oz (100–125 g) mushrooms, finely sliced
2 tablespoons (2 × 15 ml spoons) soy sauce
4 tablespoons (4 × 15 ml spoons) chicken stock
1 teaspoon (1 × 5 ml spoon) caster sugar
1 lb (450 g) tagliatelle

Put the oil in the bottom of a wok or large frying pan over a medium heat. Add the garlic, ginger, onion and a pinch of salt. After a minute, add the steak and 'stir-fry', turning the meat continuously with a wooden spoon or spatula until all visible surfaces are brown. (This should only take 2–3 minutes.) Add the Brussels sprouts and continue to stir-fry for another couple of minutes. Add the mushrooms for another minute, and finally add the soy sauce, chicken stock and caster sugar. Stir-fry for another 3–4 minutes.

Meanwhile, cook the pasta in plenty of salted, boiling water until 'al dente', drain, and put into the wok or frying pan with the other ingredients. Cook for a few more minutes to allow the pasta to absorb some of the juices. Add pepper to taste.

Serve immediately.

Bullshot quills

Bullshot is a cocktail made from vodka and consommé. If you don't have any condensed (double strength) consommé, you can gently boil the contents of a large can of ordinary consommé until the quantity of liquid is reduced by half.

For 8–10 starter size helpings, use:

>1 × 10.4 oz (1 × 295 g) can condensed consommé
>8 oz (225 g) mushrooms, sliced
>½ pint (275 ml) single cream
>8 tablespoons (8 × 15 ml spoons) vodka
>1 lb (450 g) quills
>salt and pepper

Melt the consommé in a pan. Add the mushrooms and simmer for 5 minutes. Take off the heat and stir in first the cream and then the vodka.

Meanwhile, cook the pasta in plenty of salted, boiling water. While it is still slightly too firm to the bite, remove from the heat, drain, and return to a covered pan. Pour over the sauce, season and continue to cook over a low heat, stirring occasionally, until the pasta is ready and has absorbed quite a lot of the sauce.

Serve immediately.

Quills with ham, broad beans and cream

You can substitute peas for broad beans.

For 4 starter or 2 main course helpings, use:

6 oz (175 g) broad beans
¼ pint (150 ml) double cream
4 oz (100–125 g) ham (smoked if possible), cut into small
   pieces
salt and pepper
8 oz (225 g) quills
4 oz (100–125 g) Gruyère or Cheddar cheese, grated *or* 2 oz
   (50 g) freshly grated Parmesan cheese
grated nutmeg (optional)

Cook the beans in a little salted water until barely done. Drain,
then return to the pan with the cream, ham and seasoning, and
continue to cook gently until the sauce is heated through.

Meanwhile, cook the pasta in plenty of salted, boiling water,
until just 'al dente'. Drain, and put back into the pan with the
sauce. Add the cheese and nutmeg (if used), and continue
stirring over a very low heat for another minute or so to allow
the pasta to absorb some of the sauce and the cheese to melt.

Serve very hot.

Twists with mushrooms, ham, raw tomatoes and cheese

For 4 main course helpings, use:

> 1 oz (25 g) butter
> 4 oz (100–125 g) onions or shallots, finely sliced
> 4 oz (100–125 g) mushrooms, sliced
> 4 oz (100–125 g) ham (smoked, if possible), chopped
> ½ pint (275 ml) single cream
> 8 oz (225 g) tomatoes, skinned and coarsely chopped
> 6 oz (175 g) Gruyère or strong Cheddar cheese, grated
> salt and pepper
> 1 lb (450 g) twists

Sauté the onions or shallots in the butter in a large frying pan until softened and translucent. Add the mushrooms and the ham and sauté for another couple of minutes until the mushrooms absorb the butter and darken slightly. Stir in the cream and season to taste.

Meanwhile, cook the pasta in plenty of salted, boiling water. Drain the moment the pasta is 'al dente', and return it to the pan with the sauce. Add the tomatoes and cheese, and cook all together for a couple of minutes until the tomatoes have heated through, the cheese has melted, and the pasta has absorbed some of the sauce.

Serve immediately.

Baked tagliatelle with mushrooms, ham, broccoli and cheese

This dish is definitely not for those trying to lose weight. It is unashamedly rich and delicious – one of my favourite treats. It can be an excellent starter for a dinner party, and I would recommend using an egg pasta, or even home-made tagliatelle. (Many stores now sell fresh 'home-made' pastas.) Use half-and-half green and white tagliatelle if you can find it for a particularly pretty effect.

(The broccoli is optional – I include it as much for the colour as for the taste. You could leave it out or substitute another green vegetable.)

For 8 starter size helpings, use:

> 2 oz (50 g) butter
> 8 oz (225 g) mushrooms, finely sliced
> 6 oz (175 g) broccoli, chopped or broken into medium sized pieces
> 6 oz (175 g) ham, chopped into small pieces
> 3 oz (75–100 g) freshly grated Parmesan
> 5 oz (150 g) grated Emmenthal or 8 oz (225 g) hard cheese
> 12–14 oz (325–400 g) thin tagliatelle (or tagliatelle or small macaroni)

For the béchamel sauce

> $2\frac{1}{2}$ oz (75 g) butter
> $2\frac{1}{2}$ oz (75 g) plain flour
> $1\frac{1}{2}$ pints (875 ml) milk
> $\frac{1}{2}$ pint (275 ml) single cream (or substitute extra milk)
> 2 bay leaves (optional)
> A few black peppercorns (optional)
> $\frac{1}{2}$ onion (optional)

Sauté the mushrooms gently in 1 oz (25 g) butter. Steam the broccoli or boil in salted water for a few minutes until slightly softened but still a bright green. Drain, and toss in $\frac{1}{2}$ oz (15 g) butter.

Make the béchamel sauce following the instructions on page 144.

Meanwhile, cook the pasta in plenty of salted, boiling water until 'al dente'. (Be very careful not to overcook it: if anything, the pasta should be slightly undercooked.) Drain, and toss in the remaining ½ oz (15 g) butter.

Mix the pasta together with the mushrooms, broccoli, ham, béchamel sauce and 5 oz (150 g) of the cheese in a large bowl or in the pan in which the pasta was cooked. Pour all the mixed ingredients into an ovenproof dish, sprinkle with the remaining grated cheese, and bake in a medium oven (375°F/190°C/gas mark 5), for about 45 minutes.

Spaghetti with quick tomato sauce and bacon

This recipe is based on the 'Quick and simple tomato sauce' recipe.

For 4 main course helpings:

Make the sauce as in 'Quills with quick and simple tomato sauce' (page 60). At the last minute, add:

8 oz (225 g) bacon (preferably smoked and streaky)

Grill or fry the bacon and chop into small pieces. Mix into the tomato sauce before stirring it together with the cooked, drained pasta. Continue cooking the pasta and sauce for 2–3 minutes until it is very hot.

Serve with grated cheese on the side.

Spaghetti with bacon, aubergine, cream and cheese

This is one of my favourites as it is easy to cook, particularly tasty, yet creamy and soothing – excellent for supper for two after an arduous or stressful day.

For 2 main course helpings, use:

3 oz (75–100 g) aubergine
½ oz (15 g) butter
1 tablespoon (1 × 15 ml spoon) olive oil
2 oz (50 g) bacon, rinded and cut into small pieces
4 tablespoons (4 × 15 ml spoons) each of chicken stock and white wine, *or* 8 tablespoons (8 × 15 ml spoons) chicken stock
2 pinches chilli powder
1 egg
2 fl oz (50 ml) single cream
2 tablespoons (2 × 15 ml spoons) freshly grated Parmesan cheese
salt and pepper
8 oz (225 g) spaghetti
extra grated cheese on the side

First of all prepare the aubergine. Slice into pieces about ¼–½ inch (0.5–1 cm) thick. Spread out on a piece of kitchen paper or a clean tea towel, sprinkle with salt and leave to sweat. After 10 minutes, turn the pieces over and leave to sweat from the other side.

Fry the bacon in the butter and oil for a couple of minutes. Cut the aubergine slices into strips about ½ inch (1 cm) wide, and add them to the bacon. After a minute or so add the chicken stock and/or wine and the chilli powder. Simmer for about 5 minutes, or until the aubergine is cooked. (If the mixture is too dry, add some more liquid – wine, chicken stock or hot water.) Season.

Beat the egg with the cream in a cup until well mixed. Meanwhile, cook the pasta in plenty of salted, boiling water; drain and put back into the pan. Pour the cream and egg over the pasta, and stir over a very low heat until the egg has cooked and coated the pasta. Add the aubergine and bacon mixture, and the grated cheese.

Serve immediately, very hot, with additional grated cheese on the side.

Twists with bacon, mushrooms, courgettes and cottage cheese

This is a delicious, light but filling supper or lunch dish. (Instead of courgettes you could use another vegetable such as broccoli, cauliflower or Brussels sprouts cut into small pieces.)

For 3 main course helpings, use:

> 3 oz (75–100 g) bacon (preferably smoked, streaky), cut into small pieces
> 2 tablespoons (2 × 15 ml spoons) oil
> $\frac{1}{2}$ oz (15 g) butter
> 3 oz (75–100 g) mushrooms, sliced
> 8 oz (225 g) courgettes, sliced
> 1 clove garlic, crushed
> 8 oz (225 g) cottage cheese
> 1–2 tablespoons (1–2 × 15 ml spoons) fresh chopped herbs
> _or_ $\frac{1}{2}$ tablespoon ($\frac{1}{2}$ × 15 ml spoon) dried herbs (e.g. oregano or sage)
> salt and pepper
> 10–12 oz (275–350 g) twists

Sauté the bacon in the oil and butter until browned. Add the mushrooms, courgettes and crushed garlic, and continue cooking over a gentle heat until the mushrooms have slightly softened and darkened, and the courgettes have begun to darken but are still crisp. Stir in the cottage cheese, herbs and seasoning and remove from the heat for the moment. (Don't worry if the cottage cheese all but disappears.)

Meanwhile, cook the pasta in plenty of salted, boiling water until 'al dente'. Drain and put back into the pan with the sauce. Continue stirring over the heat for a couple of minutes.

Serve immediately.

Rigatoni with bacon, mushrooms, olives and vegetables

This dish is delicious, colourful, unusual and a good choice for a relaxed supper with a few friends. Serve it with a good mixed salad, and follow it with a light dessert such as sorbet or fruit salad.

The olives give the dish its unusual flavour so it is worth finding some tasty ones, green or black. Although the recipe includes cream, this is largely absorbed by the pasta and the dish is not as rich as its ingredients might suggest.

(Other vegetables – French beans, carrots, cauliflower, leeks etc. – can be substituted for courgettes and broccoli.)

For 6 main course helpings, use:

1 oz (25 g) butter
2 tablespoons (2 × 15 ml spoons) olive oil
8 oz (225 g) bacon (preferably smoked, streaky), cut into small pieces
8 oz (225 g) mushrooms, sliced
15 olives, pitted and sliced
6 oz (175 g) courgettes, sliced
6 oz (175 g) broccoli, chopped into small pieces
6 tablespoons (6 × 15 ml spoons) white wine
½ pint (275 ml) double cream
salt and pepper
3 oz (75–100 g) grated Parmesan cheese *or* 6 oz (175 g) grated Cheddar or Leicester cheese
1 lb 5 oz (600 g) rigatoni

Sauté the bacon in the oil and butter until browned. Add the mushrooms and olives and continue cooking until the mushrooms darken and soften. Stir in the courgettes and broccoli and continue to sauté for 2–3 minutes, stirring well. Add the wine and continue cooking for a few minutes until the vegetables are almost cooked – still crunchy and green, but not actually rabbit-food raw! Stir in the cream and season to taste.

Meanwhile cook the pasta until 'al dente' in plenty of salted, boiling water. Drain, and mix together with the sauce and grated cheese over a low heat for a couple of minutes.

Serve very hot with extra cheese on the side if you like.

Spaghetti with eggs, bacon, cream and mushrooms – Spaghetti alla carbonara (with mushrooms)

This is another excellent 'storecupboard' dish. It is perfect for a Sunday night supper in front of the television, easy to prepare and very popular.

(Instead of bacon, you can use finely chopped ham or salami, or lightly fried calves' liver or cooked kidney cut into small pieces. Mushrooms are not used in the traditional Italian dish, and can be left out of this recipe.)

For 2 main course helpings, use:

>1 oz (25 g) butter
>*6 oz (175 g) bacon
>2 eggs
>¼ pint (150 ml) single or double cream
>4 oz (100–125 g) mushrooms, sliced
>salt and pepper
>8 oz (225 g) spaghetti (or quills)
>grated cheese (optional)

Remove the rind from the bacon, then gently fry it in ½ oz (15 g) butter until just beginning to crisp. Remove from the pan to the chopping board and, when cool enough, cut into small pieces. Meanwhile, in the same pan, cook the mushrooms until softened.

Beat the eggs, cream and seasoning together in a cup or bowl and put aside.

Meanwhile, cook the pasta in plenty of salted, boiling water until 'al dente'. Drain and return to the pan. Add the remaining butter and melt it into the pasta over a low heat. Return the bacon to the mushroom pan and reheat gently. Pour the cream sauce over the pasta and *stir well* – the eggs in the sauce will cook when they come into contact with the hot pasta but will

* I use fairly lean, smoked bacon

turn into 'scrambled eggs' at the bottom of the pan if you do not stir the mixture thoroughly enough.

Remove from the heat and stir in the bacon and mushrooms.

Serve immediately, very hot, with grated cheese on the side.

Baked quills with leeks, chicken and mushrooms

For 6–8 main course helpings, use:

For the chicken and mushroom mixture

>1 medium chicken (3½ lb approx.)
>2 bay leaves
>10 peppercorns
>1 small onion, peeled and quartered
>1½ oz (25–50 g) butter
>12 oz (325–350 g) mushrooms, sliced
>1 clove garlic, crushed
>grated nutmeg (to taste)
>salt and pepper

For the leek filling

>2 oz (50 g) butter
>7 oz (200 g) onion, finely sliced
>2 cloves garlic, crushed
>1½ lb (675 g) leeks, washed and sliced
>¼ pint (150 ml) chicken stock (reserved from the liquid in which the chicken is cooked)

For the béchamel sauce

>2 oz (50 g) butter
>2 oz (50 g) flour
>1 pint (575 ml) milk
>1 teaspoon (1 × 5 ml spoon) mustard powder
>½ teaspoon (1 × 2.5 ml spoon) curry powder

Other ingredients

>18 oz (500 g) quills (or macaroni or tagliatelle)
>3 oz (75–100 g) Gruyère, Emmenthal or grated Cheddar cheese

Poach the chicken in water with the bay leaves, peppercorns and onion for about an hour, or until the chicken comes away from the bone quite easily. Remove the chicken from the pot and reserve the liquid. Take the meat off the bone, discarding the skin, chop the meat into smallish pieces and put aside. Sauté the mushrooms together with the garlic in the butter, until the mushrooms have softened and darkened. Add the chicken, salt and pepper and some grated nutmeg, and cook together for another few minutes. Put aside.

To make the leek filling, first sauté the onion and garlic in the butter until soft. Stir in the leeks, add a little of the chicken stock, and simmer in a covered pan for 20 minutes, stirring occasionally and gradually adding the rest of the $\frac{1}{4}$ pint (150 ml) chicken stock. Put aside.

Make the béchamel sauce with the ingredients listed following the instructions on page 144.

Meanwhile, cook the pasta in plenty of salted, boiling water until 'al dente'. Drain, and put back into the pan. Add the chicken and mushroom mixture and the béchamel sauce, and mix well.

Take an ovenproof dish – a roasting tin about 15 × 11 inches (38 × 28 cms) is quite a good size. Spread all the leek mixture evenly across the bottom. Cover with the mixture of pasta, chicken and béchamel sauce and sprinkle the grated cheese on top. Bake, covered with foil, in a hot oven (400°F/200°C/gas mark 6) for about 1 hour. Remove the foil for the last 20 minutes to allow the cheese to brown.

Note: You can make this dish a day in advance and leave it in the fridge covered with foil until you are ready to cook it. If it then appears a little dry on top, pour an extra $\frac{1}{4}$ pint (150 ml) single cream over the whole dish.

Twists with ginger, chicken, cream and cheese

This is a good recipe for using up leftover scraps of cold chicken.
You can use another cold meat, or a combination of meats – I find chicken and tongue together quite delicious.

For 4 main course helpings, use:

2 tablespoons (2 × 15 ml spoons) olive oil
2 teaspoons (2 × 5 ml spoons) fresh ginger, peeled and chopped
4–6 oz (100–175 g) cooked chicken, tongue, ham (or a combination of these or other cooked meats), cut into smallish pieces
½ pint (275 ml) single cream
salt and pepper
1 lb (450 g) twists
4 oz (100–125 g) Gruyère or Emmenthal cheese, grated
pinch of cayenne pepper (optional)

Sauté the ginger in the oil in a large pan over a low heat for a minute. Add the meats, and sauté for another couple of minutes, stirring well to distribute the chopped ginger. Add the cream and seasoning.

Meanwhile, cook the pasta in plenty of salted, boiling water. Drain, and return to the pan. Mix in the sauce, the grated cheese and a sprinkling of cayenne pepper, and continue stirring over a low heat until the cheese has melted.

Serve immediately.

Wholewheat pasta tubes with chicken, cream, mushrooms, mustard and Gruyère cheese

Another useful recipe for using up left-over chicken or turkey.

For 3 main course helpings, use:

  2 tablespoons (2 × 15 ml spoons) olive oil *or* 1 oz (25 g)
   butter
  8 oz (225 g) onion, sliced
  2 cloves garlic, crushed
  6–8 oz (175–225 g) cold cooked chicken, cut into small
   pieces
  4 oz (100–125 g) mushrooms, sliced
  1 wine glass (4 fl oz/125 ml) white wine
  ¼ pint (150 ml) single cream
  1 teaspoon (1 × 5 ml spoon) Dijon, French or German
   mustard
  grated nutmeg (to taste)
  salt and pepper
  12 oz (325–350 g) wholewheat pasta tubes
  4 oz (100–125 g) Gruyère cheese, grated (or substitute
   Emmenthal, Jarlsberg or Cheddar)

Put the onion, garlic and oil into a small casserole. Cook in the oven at a very low temperature (275°F/140°C/gas mark 1) for 45 minutes, stirring occasionally. Remove the casserole from the oven, stir in the chicken, mushrooms and wine, and continue to cook over a low heat on top of the stove, stirring occasionally, to allow the chicken to absorb some of the liquids. Add the cream, mustard, nutmeg, salt and pepper, and stew gently for another 6–7 minutes.

Meanwhile, cook the pasta in plenty of salted, boiling water. Drain and put back into the pan, or into a heated serving dish. Pour on the sauce and half the cheese, and mix together well. Serve immediately with the rest of the cheese on the side.

Spaghetti with a mild curried chicken sauce and tomato

For 4 main course helpings, use:

4 tablespoons (4 × 15 ml spoons) oil (preferably ½ sunflower, ½ olive oil)
8 oz (225 g) onion, sliced
2 cloves garlic, crushed
1 tablespoon (1 × 15 ml spoon) curry powder
12 oz (325–350 g) uncooked chicken, cut into small pieces
1 tablespoon (1 × 15 ml spoon) flour
6 tablespoons (6 × 15 ml spoons) apple juice *or* white wine
¾ pint (425 ml) chicken stock (fresh or made with a cube)
6 tablespoons (6 × 15 ml spoons) single cream
salt and pepper
12 oz (325–350 g) tomatoes, skinned and coarsely chopped
1 lb (450 g) spaghetti (or pasta tubes)
2 tablespoons (2 × 15 ml spoons) fresh, chopped coriander or parsley (optional)

Sauté the onion and the garlic in the oil until softened and translucent. Stir in the curry powder, then add the chicken pieces. Sauté until the chicken is cooked on the outside, then stir in the flour and the apple juice or wine. Add the chicken stock gradually, and simmer for about 5–10 minutes or until the chicken is fully cooked. Stir in the cream, the seasoning, and at the last moment add the tomatoes, allowing them just to heat through but not cook.

Meanwhile, cook the pasta in plenty of salted, boiling water until 'al dente', drain and put into a preheated serving dish. Mix in the sauce and sprinkle the fresh herbs on top.

Serve immediately.

Tagliatelle with spicy chicken livers

This is a satisfying dish, and easy and quick to cook.

For 2 main course helpings, use:

> 1 oz (25 g) butter
> 1 tablespoon (1 × 15 ml spoon) oil
> 4 oz (100–125 g) onions or shallots, finely chopped
> 1–2 cloves garlic, crushed
> ¼ teaspoon (½ × 2.5 ml spoon) garam masala
> 2 pinches chilli powder (to taste)
> ½ teaspoon (1 × 2.5 ml spoon) ground coriander
> 8 oz (225 g) chicken livers, chopped into pieces about ½–1
>   inch (1–3 cm) square
> 1 wine glass (4 fl oz/125 ml) wine
> ½ pint (275 ml) chicken stock (made with ½ cube)
> salt and pepper
> 8 oz (225 g) tagliatelle

Melt the butter with the oil in a heavy frying pan. Sauté the onions and garlic over a low heat until the onions turn soft and golden. Stir in the herbs and spices, and then add the chicken livers, turning the pieces with a wooden spoon until well browned on the outsides. Pour in the wine, and allow the liquids to bubble for a minute. Then add the chicken stock, a little at a time, and continue cooking until the livers are fully done (about 10–12 minutes), stirring to ensure they do not stick to the bottom of the pan. Season to taste.

Meanwhile, cook the pasta in plenty of boiling, salted water. Drain, and put into a preheated serving dish with an extra knob of butter (about ½ oz/15 g). Allow the butter to melt on the hot pasta, stirring it in with a wooden spoon, then pour the spicy chicken liver sauce on top.

Serve very hot.

Macaroni mixed grill

If you don't have all the main ingredients for this, just use a little more of one of the other ingredients. This dish is *not* for those who worry about their cholesterol intake!

For 4 main course helpings, use:

> 2 large pork sausages (*or* 4 small chipolatas)
> 2 rashers lean bacon
> 1 oz (25 g) butter
> 2 lambs' kidneys, chopped into pieces about ½ inch (1 cm) square
> 4 oz (100–125 g) mushrooms, sliced
> 6 tablespoons (6 × 15 ml spoons) single cream
> 1 egg
> salt and pepper
> grated nutmeg (optional)
> 14–16 oz (400–450 g) large pasta tubes (macaroni, rigatoni or quills)

Grill the sausages and the bacon. While they are cooking, melt the butter in a frying pan and add the kidneys. Cook them over a low heat, turning with a wooden spoon until all the pieces are browned on the outside. Add the mushrooms, and continue to cook until softened. Slice the grilled sausages and bacon and add them to the contents of the frying pan. Pour on half the cream, and cook for a couple of minutes to allow the juices to integrate with the cream. Mix the remaining cream with the beaten egg in a cup, and add the seasoning and nutmeg.

Meanwhile, cook the pasta in plenty of salted, boiling water. Drain, and return to the saucepan. Pour the cream-and-egg mixture over the pasta and stir well. The egg will cook in the heat as it comes in contact with the hot pasta which will be coated with the mixture. Stir in all the remaining ingredients, and return the pan to a low heat for a minute or two, stirring all the time.

Fish dishes

COOKING AND SERVING PASTA

Choice of pasta

You don't have to use the pasta type specified in a particular recipe, but if you want to use another type bear in mind that as a general rule it is best to substitute one pasta type with another of similar characteristics (see page 8).

Timing

The time needed for pasta to cook can vary so much that I have not specified cooking times in the recipes. Aim to have the pasta ready at the same time as the sauce, and test it frequently as it nears the 'al dente' stage (see pages 2–4).

Serve it *hot*!

Hot pasta dishes should be served while they are still *very* hot. Always preheat plates and serving dishes.

'Cheese on the side'

Not all pasta are improved by adding grated cheese. Serve it as a side dish to be added only if needed – *after* tasting.

Seafood and mushroom lasagne

For 6 main course helpings, use:

For the seafood filling

> *1½ lb (675 g) cod, or another white fish, cut into large pieces
> 6 oz (175 g) cooked, shelled prawns
> ½ pint (275 ml) milk
> ½ pint (275 ml) water
> 2 bay leaves
> 1 wine glass (4 fl oz/125 ml) white wine
> 3 oz (75–100 g) carrot, grated or julienned
> ½ pint (275 ml) single cream

For the mushroom filling

> 2 oz (50 g) butter
> 6 oz (175 g) onion, finely sliced
> 1 lb (450 g) mushrooms, sliced

For the béchamel sauce

> 1 oz (25 g) butter
> 1 oz (25 g) flour
> milk and water mixture in which you have poached the cod,
>   made up to one pint with milk

Additional ingredients

> ¼ pint (150 ml) single cream
> 2 oz (50 g) grated Parmesan or Emmenthal cheese
> 1 lb (450 g) lasagne
> salt and pepper

Poach the white fish in the milk and water with the bay leaves.
Allow to simmer for five minutes before removing from the heat
and cooling slightly. Then remove the fish from the pan with a

* Buy extra fish if they are small, as more will be wasted in skin and
bones.

slotted spoon and discard the skin and bones. Strain the poaching liquid into a measuring jug and make up to 1 pint (575 ml) with extra milk.

Return the fish to the pan with the grated carrot, pour over the wine and heat until the wine bubbles. Add the cream and the prawns and poach gently for another 5 minutes on a low heat, stirring occasionally. Season to taste, remove from the heat and allow to cool.

Sauté the onions in the butter on a very low heat for 10 minutes, until they are well softened. Add the mushrooms and sauté for another few minutes.

Make a thin béchamel sauce with the ingredients listed, following the instructions on page 144.

Cook the lasagne as instructed on pages 4–5.

Now take a fairly shallow ovenproof dish, 3–4 inch. (7.5–10 cm) deep, and butter it well. Spread a very thin layer of the fish mixture in the bottom of the dish, followed by a layer of lasagne, a thin layer of mushroom mixture, and finally a couple of tablespoons of the béchamel sauce. Seasoning well between each layer, continue in layers until you have finished all the ingredients. (I find I can usually manage 2 layers of each filling.) Spread the remaining béchamel sauce on the top, pour over the cream, and sprinkle with the cheese.

Cover the dish in foil to help the lasagne absorb the juices and cook in a fairly hot oven (400°F/200°C/gas mark 6) for about an hour, removing the foil for the last 15–30 minutes cooking time, at the same time moving the dish to the top of the oven to allow the cheese topping to brown.

If you are not ready to eat exactly on time, the dish can sit very happily in the oven for an extra half hour at a lower temperature.

Quills with monkfish, cream and curry

You can add a little cooked vegetable to this dish, stirring it in just before serving. Add 4 oz (100–125 g) sliced mushrooms sautéd in ½ oz (15 g) butter, for example, or 4 oz (100–125 g) steamed broccoli, mange-tout peas or courgettes, tossed in ½ oz (15 g) butter.

For 4 starter or 2 main course helpings, use:

1 oz (25 g) butter
4 oz (100–125 g) onion, finely sliced
6 oz (175 g) monkfish, cut into small pieces
5 tablespoons (5 × 15 ml spoons) white wine
¼ teaspoon (½ × 2.5 ml spoon) curry powder
2 teaspoons (2 × 5 ml spoons) plain flour
4 tablespoons (4 × 15 ml spoons) milk
6 tablespoons (6 × 15 ml spoons) single cream
salt and pepper
8 oz (225 g) quills

Sauté the onion in the butter over a low heat until the onion is softened and translucent. Add the monkfish pieces, and continue to sauté for a couple of minutes. Stir in the wine, curry powder and flour, and allow to cook for a minute. Finally add the milk, cream and seasoning and continue to stir over a low heat until the fish is cooked.

Meanwhile, cook the pasta in plenty of salted, boiling water until 'al dente'. Drain and return to the pan or a preheated serving dish, and stir in the sauce.

Serve immediately.

Note: If you need to reheat the sauce before mixing it in with the pasta, you may need to add a little extra milk or cream as it tends to thicken if left waiting.

Quills with carrots, scallops, vodka and peas – Penne Traviata

'Penne Traviata' is living proof that preparing pasta is easy and can be done in the face of all distractions. While I was in the throes of creating this dish one of my dinner guests, an American friend Mossa Bildner (who happens to be a wonderful opera singer) took it into her head to amuse herself by singing along with my tape of *La Traviata* (Act II). She enacted all roles and every aspect of the plot, throwing herself headlong on to the kitchen floor as a weeping Violetta, pulling herself up by the legs of the kitchen table to portray Alfredo, leaping suddenly to her feet with a stage whispered 'this is where Violetta *has* to stop weeping and get up, or she can't possibly hit the high notes!'

For 4 generous starter or 2–3 main course helpings, use:

½ oz (15 g) butter
1 clove garlic, sliced or crushed
4 oz (100–125 g) onion, finely sliced
6 oz (175 g) carrots, quite finely chopped
6 tablespoons (6 × 15 ml spoons) apple or orange juice
4 oz (100–125 g) frozen peas (petits pois)
4 oz (100–125 g) cottage cheese
¼ pint (150 ml) single cream
4 tablespoons (4 × 15 ml spoons) vodka
salt and pepper
10–12 oz (275–350 g) quills
grated Parmesan cheese

Melt the butter in a small casserole. Add the onion and garlic, give it a good stir with a wooden spoon, and put into a very low oven (250°F/130°C/gas mark ½) for 30 minutes, stirring occasionally. Return the casserole to the top of the stove on a low heat, and add the carrots, then the fruit juice. Replace the lid and allow to simmer for 5 minutes. Stir in the peas, replace the lid and simmer for another 10 minutes. (If at any point the liquid dries up and the ingredients start sticking to the bottom of the pan, add a little water.) Stir in the cottage cheese, allow it to melt a little, and then stir in the cream and the vodka. Season.

Meanwhile, cook the pasta in plenty of salted, boiling water until 'al dente'. Drain, and put back into the pan or into a preheated serving dish. Stir in the sauce.

Serve immediately with grated Parmesan cheese on the side.

Tagliatelle with salmon, mushrooms and cream

This is a very good recipe for using up any leftover salmon or salmon trout.

For 4 main course helpings, use:

1½ oz (25–50 g) butter
8 oz (225 g) mushrooms, sliced
6–8 oz (175–225 g) cooked salmon, in small pieces
½ pint (275 ml) single cream
salt and pepper
1 lb (450 g) tagliatelle

Sauté the mushrooms in the butter until softened. Add the cooked salmon, cream and seasoning and continue cooking on a low heat for another 2–3 minutes.

Meanwhile, cook the pasta in plenty of salted, boiling water until 'al dente'. Drain, mix with the sauce, and put into a preheated serving dish.

Serve very hot.

Spaghetti with smoked salmon and cream

Some fishmongers, delicatessen shops, and even some super-markets, sell smoked salmon offcuts at a vastly reduced price, so this dish need not be as extravagant as it may seem.

For 4 starter size helpings, use:

4–6 oz (100–175 g) smoked salmon or smoked salmon trout pieces
½ pint (275 ml) single cream
8 oz (225 g) spaghetti (or spaghettini)
salt and pepper
½ oz (15 g) butter

Put the smoked salmon pieces into a bowl with the cream and set aside.

Cook the pasta in plenty of salted, boiling water. Drain, and put back into the pan over a very low heat with the butter and seasoning, stirring with a wooden spoon until the butter has melted. Strain the cream, now salmon-flavoured, into the pasta and allow it to heat through. Add the smoked salmon at the last moment before serving to ensure it does not cook and go mushy, so losing its delicate and delicious quality.

Butterflies with fresh salmon, boiled eggs and cream

Another excellent use for any left-over cold salmon!

For 4 main course servings, use:

> 1 oz (25 g) butter
> 3 oz (75–100 g) carrots, grated
> 3 tablespoons (3 × 15 ml spoons) white wine (optional)
> 6–8 oz (175–225 g) cooked salmon, flaked off the bone
> 4 hard-boiled eggs, chopped or mashed
> ½ pint (275 ml) single cream
> 1 lb (450 g) butterflies

Sauté the grated carrot in the butter for a couple of minutes until softened, then pour in the wine (if used) and allow to bubble for a minute. Add the salmon, eggs and then the cream and mix well together.

Meanwhile, cook the pasta in plenty of salted, boiling water. Drain, and put into a preheated serving dish. Pour on the sauce and mix well.

Serve immediately.

Quills with smoked salmon, vodka and cream

This is a particularly delicious dish, simple and luxurious.

For 8 starter size helpings, use:

12 oz (325–350 g) smoked salmon (offcuts)
½ pint (275 ml) double cream
9 tablespoons (9 × 15 ml spoons) vodka
salt and pepper
1 tablespoon (1 × 15 ml spoon) chopped fresh dill (if
    available)
1 lb (450 g) quills

Cut the smoked salmon into little pieces and put aside.

Cook the pasta in plenty of salted, boiling water until 'al dente'. Drain, and put back into the pan or a preheated serving dish. At the last moment, heat the vodka and cream until almost boiling. (Take care not to let it boil over as it might catch fire. This happened to me once – it was not serious, just surprising!) Mix the cream, vodka and smoked salmon into the hot pasta.

Serve immediately.

Note: All the above needs to be done extremely quickly, so that the pasta and sauce remain hot but the smoked salmon does not cook.

Twists with salmon, monkfish and prawns

This dish is one of my favourites – delicate, very delicious and pretty to look at. It makes an excellent starter for a special occasion, and is surprisingly easy and straightforward to prepare. You could substitute another firm, white fish for the monkfish, and alter the proportions of the three fish according to availability and price. If you buy the fish from a fishmonger, ask him to give you some extra scraps for boiling up with the court bouillon: part of the success of this dish depends on a fairly rich fish stock.

For 6–8 starter size helpings, use:

For the court bouillon

> ¾ pint (425 ml) water
> 1 tablespoon (1 × 15 ml spoon) wine vinegar *or* 2
>   tablespoons (2 × 15 ml spoons) wine
> 10 peppercorns (approx.)
> 2 bay leaves

Other ingredients

> 8 oz (225 g) salmon, weighed with skin and bone
> 6 oz (175 g) monkfish, weighed with skin and bone
> 1½ oz (25–50 g) butter
> 4 oz (100–125 g) leeks or onion, finely chopped
> 4 oz (100–125 g) carrots, chopped
> 6 fl oz (175 ml) dry white wine
> 8 fl oz (225 ml) double cream
> 12–16 oz (325–450 g) twists (or another fairly small or
>   delicate pasta shape)
> 2 oz (50 g) shelled, cooked prawns
> salt and pepper

Put the ingredients for the court bouillon into a large saucepan and add the salmon and monkfish so that the fish is completely covered. Bring to the boil and simmer for 2 minutes. Remove the pan from the heat and transfer the fish to a plate using a slotted spoon. When the fish is cool enough to handle, remove the skin and any bone, and cut into medium-sized chunks, about 1 inch (2.5 cms) square. Don't worry if the fish is not yet completely cooked.

Put the skin and bones back into the saucepan with the court bouillon (plus any other fish scraps), and continue to boil gently for about 20 minutes, reducing the liquid a little. Strain the liquid, and make it up to 8 fl oz (225 ml) with water. (If you have too much liquid, continue to boil it until it reduces sufficiently.) Put aside.

Sauté the leeks or onion and the carrots in the butter until softened (about 4 minutes). Pour in half the wine, bring to the boil and then remove immediately from the heat. Pour in the fish stock, the remaining wine and the cream, stir, and put aside until the pasta is ready.

Meanwhile, cook the pasta in plenty of salted, boiling water until only just 'al dente' – almost a little undercooked. Drain and put into an ovenproof dish, mixing in a little oil or a small knob of butter to keep the pasta from sticking. Add all the fish, including the prawns, to the pan containing the sauce and heat up until very hot but not boiling. Mix the sauce into the pasta with a wooden spoon, cover the dish tightly with foil and place in a medium oven (375°F/190°C/gas mark 5) for 20 minutes, turning the pasta over with a wooden spoon after 10 minutes to ensure that it all has a chance to be immersed in sauce and to absorb some. If by any chance the mixture seems too dry, add a little more cream and white wine.

Serve very hot, *without* cheese!

Kate's shells with tuna fish, lemon and peas

Kate Fletcher is the brave and loyal friend without whose help this book might never have been finished Over the several months it took to prepare the recipes for publication, she patiently typed, organized, spotted inconsistencies, advised, and was a constant and enthusiastic support. She has become known as Superwoman. When we started work on the book she was already looking after her house, her husband and their baby daughter, Hannah. Halfway through she gave birth to a son, took a few hours off and was back to work the next day. I can only suppose she holds a baby under each arm and types with her toes.

For 4 main course helpings, use:

>2 oz (50 g) butter
>2 oz (50 g) flour
>$\frac{3}{4}$ pint (425 ml) milk
>juice of 1 lemon
>ground black pepper
>4 oz (100–125 g) frozen peas
>6$\frac{1}{2}$ oz (185 g) tin tuna fish, drained
>1 lb (450 g) shells (or other pasta shapes)

Melt the butter in a pan over a low heat. Stir in the flour and cook for 1–2 minutes. Increase the heat, and add the milk little by little, stirring all the time to make a thick white sauce. Add the lemon juice, black pepper (to taste) and frozen peas (straight from the freezer). Allow the peas to cook in the sauce for a few minutes, then stir in the tuna fish, breaking it up with the wooden spoon and allowing it to heat through.

Meanwhile, cook the pasta in plenty of salted, boiling water until 'al dente'. Drain the pasta, then put it back into the pan or into a preheated serving dish and stir in the sauce.

Serve immediately.

Pasta tubes with tuna fish, avocado and courgettes

A quick, light and fresh dish, excellent for a summer lunch or supper. I like to serve it hot or warm, but it can also be eaten cold. (You can use broccoli instead of courgettes.)

For 3 main course helpings, use:

2 tablespoons (2 × 15 ml spoons) olive oil
8 oz (225 g) courgettes, finely sliced
3½ oz (99 g) tin tuna fish, drained
1 ripe avocado, medium to large, sliced into smallish pieces
10–12 oz (275–350 g) pasta tubes

For the vinaigrette

1 tablespoon (1 × 15 ml spoon) wine vinegar
3 tablespoons (3 × 15 ml spoons) olive oil
1 teaspoon (1 × 5 ml spoon) mustard (French or German) *or*
   ½ teaspoon (1 × 2.5 ml spoon) English mustard
½ teaspoon (1 × 2.5 ml spoon) caster sugar
salt and pepper

Sauté the courgettes or broccoli in the oil until lightly browned but still crisp. Mix the vinaigrette ingredients in a cup, beating well with a fork.

Meanwhile, cook the pasta in plenty of salted, boiling water until 'al dente'. Drain, and put into a bowl with the vegetable, tuna fish and avocado. Pour over the vinaigrette and mix well.

Serve immediately.

Note: This dish does not really need cheese, but if you want you could serve some grated Parmesan, Cheddar or Leicester on the side.

Spaghetti with tuna fish and anchovies

This is a particularly tasty and popular dish. Provided you keep the ingredients in store, it is easy to make on the spur of the moment. The olives are not essential if you don't happen to have any handy.

For 4 starter or 2 main course helpings, use:

> 3 tablespoons (3 × 15 ml spoons) olive oil
> 4 oz (100–125 g) onion, finely sliced
> 2 cloves garlic, crushed
> 8 anchovies, coarsely chopped
> 8 olives, halved and pitted
> pinch chilli powder (optional)
> herbs to taste, e.g. 1 tablespoon (1 × 15 ml spoon) fresh coriander, or $\frac{1}{2}$ tablespoon ($\frac{1}{2}$ × 15 ml spoon) dried oregano
> $6\frac{1}{2}$ oz (185 g) tin tuna fish, drained
> 4 tablespoons (4 × 15 ml spoons) white wine, or chicken stock or water
> salt and pepper
> 8 oz (225 g) spaghetti (or another pasta)
> $\frac{1}{2}$ oz (15 g) butter

Sauté the onions and garlic in the oil over a very low heat, taking care not to let the garlic burn. Add the anchovies and continue cooking until they disintegrate. Stir in the olives, chilli powder and herbs (if used) and the tuna fish. Break the tuna fish up with a wooden spoon, and continue cooking for a few minutes, adding the wine or chicken stock gradually. Increase the amount of wine, stock or water used if the sauce appears too dry. Season.

Meanwhile, cook the pasta in plenty of boiling, salted water. Drain and return to the pan. Stir in the butter, and then the sauce.

Serve immediately.

Spaghetti with tuna fish, tomatoes, anchovies and olives

This dish is extremely tasty, easy to prepare, and a good 'out of the storecupboard' standby.

For 6–8 starter or 4 main course helpings, use:

3 tablespoons (3 × 15 ml spoons) olive oil
1 large clove garlic, crushed
4 oz (100–125 g) onion, finely sliced
3 anchovy fillets, coarsely chopped
2 pinches chilli powder (optional, to taste)
10 olives (preferably black), halved and pitted
6½ oz (185 g) tin tuna fish, drained
2 tablespoons (2 × 15 ml spoons) white wine
1 teaspoon (1 × 5 ml spoon) dried oregano
14 oz (400 g) tinned Italian tomatoes
¼ pint (125 ml) chicken stock (fresh, or made with ¼ cube)
1 lb (450 g) spaghetti (or macaroni)
Extra grated cheese on the side (if you *must*!)

In a large frying pan sauté the garlic and onion in the oil over a low heat. Stir in the chilli powder, if used. After a minute, stir in the anchovies, and continue to sauté until they have disintegrated. Add the olives, tuna fish and white wine, stirring together continuously with a wooden spoon. Next add the tomatoes, breaking them up with the spoon. Season, then cover the pan and simmer on a low heat for 30 minutes. (Cooking for this length of time enriches the flavour, though if you are very short of time you could shorten the simmering period.) Every 5 minutes or so, remove the lid from the pan to stir the sauce and to add the chicken stock bit by bit.

Meanwhile, cook the pasta in plenty of salted, boiling water until 'al dente'. Drain the pasta, then return it to the pan or put it into a preheated serving dish, and mix the sauce in well.

Serve immediately.

Cold macaroni with tuna fish, anchovies, capers, cheese and mayonnaise

This cold pasta dish is fairly rich and very delicious. The capers and tuna give it its flavour, so don't worry if you have to leave out the celery, anchovies or fresh herbs, or if you have to substitute a different cheese. You can add 4 oz (100–125 g) chopped ham to the mixture if you like.

Although the idea for this recipe was suggested by an Italian friend, I have tasted something very similar in a Japanese restaurant, served as a starter.

For 6 starter or salad-size helpings, use:

$6\frac{1}{2}$ oz (185 g) tin tuna fish
1 tablespoon (1 × 15 ml spoon) capers, chopped
6 anchovy fillets, soaked in milk, then drained and coarsely chopped
3 oz (75–100 g) celery, chopped into small slices
4 oz (100–125 g) Gruyère cheese, chopped into small cubes
7 oz (200 g) mayonnaise (I use Hellmanns bottled mayonnaise)
1 tablespoon (1 × 15 ml spoon) olive oil
1 tablespoon (1 × 15 ml spoon) lemon juice
2 tablespoons (2 × 15 ml spoons) chopped fresh herbs, e.g. basil or chives (optional)
9 oz (250 g) small macaroni (or small shells)

Drain the oil from the tinned tuna fish and break the fish up into a bowl large enough to take all the ingredients – including the cooked pasta. Add the other ingredients and stir together. Cook the pasta in plenty of salted, boiling water until 'al dente'. Drain in a colander, and rinse in cold water to cool it and prevent it from cooking any further. Mix into the other ingredients, cover the bowl and leave for a few hours before serving.

Bows with spicy fish fingers and tomato sauce

This dish is economical, tasty and very quick and easy to make. You can also throw in a few black olives or capers if you have some handy.

For 2 main course helpings, use:

2 fish fingers
½ oz (15 g) butter
1 clove garlic, crushed
3 oz (75–100 g) onion, finely sliced
*½–1 dried red chilli, chopped into small pieces *or* ¼
   teaspoon (½ × 2.5 ml spoon) chilli powder
1 tablespoon (1 × 15 ml spoon) tomato purée
¼ pint (150 ml) chicken stock made with ¼ cube in hot water
1 tablespoon (1 × 15 ml spoon) olive oil
8 oz (225 g) bows

Grill the fish fingers until lightly browned and soft. Chop coarsely. Meanwhile, gently sauté the garlic and onion in the butter. Stir in the chilli, and then the chopped fish fingers. Add the tomato purée and the chicken stock, and gently simmer for about 3 minutes, adding more liquid if the sauce appears too dry. Season.
   Meanwhile, cook the pasta in plenty of salted, boiling water. Drain, and put back into the pan. Stir in the tablespoon of oil, and then the sauce – making sure it is well integrated with the pasta.
   Serve very hot.

* The amount of chilli used is always according to taste. You may wish to leave it out entirely. When I make this dish I use a very small, whole dried red chilli – but I like my food very spicy!

Quills with kipper sauce

The idea of combining kippers with pasta was first suggested to me by Willie Landels and this recipe is the resulting adaptation. Willie is Italian, and his attitude to pasta perfectly illustrates my theory that if you were to move the population of Italy to England tomorrow they would *not* sit around bemoaning the lack of Pecorino cheese or fresh plum tomatoes. Instead they would set to work concocting delicious pasta dishes out of local English produce.

This dish is not as overpowering as it might appear. The blandness of the pasta absorbs some of the 'kipperishness', leaving the sauce still extremely tasty. It is not a particularly colourful dish, so serve it with a bright mixed salad or a fresh green vegetable.

For 2 main course helpings, use:

> 3 tablespoons (3 × 15 ml spoons) olive oil
> 1 clove garlic, crushed
> 3 oz (75–100 g) onion, finely sliced
> 4 oz (100–125 g) cooked kipper, boned and mashed
> ½ teaspoon (1 × 2.5 ml spoon) dried sage (or another herb, either dried, or fresh and chopped)
> salt and pepper
> 7 oz (200 g) quills

Gently sauté the garlic and onion in the oil over a low heat. Add the kipper and dried sage and continue to sauté for a couple of minutes.

Meanwhile, cook the pasta in plenty of salted, boiling water. Drain, and mix with the sauce.

Note: I used tinned kipper fillets, which worked well and were a convenient and easy alternative to fresh kippers. Frozen, cook-in-the-bag kippers are also handy. If you are using fresh kippers, allow about 8 oz (225 g) starting weight. Grill or poach the kippers, debone and skin them, then flake or mash the fish.

Twists with quick tomato sauce and sardines

There is a traditional Italian pasta sauce incorporating sardines and tomatoes. This is a quick and easy, and very delicious, invented version based on the 'Quick and Simple Tomato Sauce' recipe.

For 4 main course helpings, use:

>   4 tablespoons (4 × 15 ml spoons) olive oil
>   1–2 cloves garlic, crushed
>   6 tablespoons (6 × 15 ml spoons) tomato purée
>   ½ pint (275 ml) chicken stock (made with 1 stock cube and
>   hot water)
>   2 teaspoons (2 × 5 ml spoons) dried herbs (oregano, sage,
>   thyme, marjoram etc.)
>   1 teaspoon (1 × 5 ml spoon) sugar
>   salt and pepper
>   13 oz (375 g) quills
>   4 oz (100–125 g) tinned sardines, boned and coarsely
>   chopped
>   a few black olives, pitted and sliced (optional)

Make the sauce as in 'Quills with quick and simple tomato sauce' (page 60).

Cook the pasta in plenty of boiling, salted water.

At the last minute, add the sardines and olives to the sauce.

Stir the sauce into the pan with the cooked, drained pasta and continue mixing over a low heat for 2–3 minutes.

Serve piping hot. It is traditional in Italy *not* to serve grated cheese with pasta sauces incorporating fish.

Spaghetti with anchovies and onions

This simple dish is quick to make and very tasty. The anchovy flavour is surprisingly subtle.

For 2 main course helpings, use:

- 3 tablespoons (3 × 15 ml spoons) olive oil
- 2 cloves garlic, crushed
- 4 oz (100–125 g) onion, chopped
- 2 pinches chilli powder
- 5 anchovy fillets, coarsely chopped
- 6 olives, pitted and chopped
- ¼ teaspoon (½ × 2.5 ml spoon) dried oregano
- 2 tablespoons (2 × 15 ml spoons) white wine (or substitute extra chicken stock)
- 4 tablespoons (4 × 15 ml spoons) chicken stock (use hot water from the pasta pot and a large pinch of stock cube)
- salt and pepper
- 8 oz (225 g) spaghetti (or spaghettini)

Sauté the onion and garlic in the oil over a low heat until softened and translucent. Stir in the chilli powder and the anchovies, and continue to cook until the anchovies start to disintegrate. Add the olives and oregano, followed by the wine, chicken stock and seasoning. Stew gently for a few minutes.

Meanwhile, cook the pasta in plenty of salted, boiling water. Drain and put back into the pan or into a preheated serving dish. Add the sauce and mix together well.

Serve very hot.

Quills with broccoli and fried anchovy breadcrumbs

Broccoli and anchovy is a traditional pasta combination in parts of southern Italy. I hope that my version, using fried anchovy breadcrumbs, is an original variation!

You could serve the pasta and broccoli sauce on its own, as originally suggested to me by the Italian composer Gian Carlo Menotti and his son Chip. Cooked by their housekeeper, Agnese, it was at the time their favourite pasta dish. When we tried it we found it to be slightly bland – more suitable as a side dish with a meat or fish course – and that the addition of anchovy breadcrumbs was a definite improvement.

For 4 starter or 2 main course helpings, use:

For the breadcrumbs

>2 tablespoons (2 × 15 ml spoons) olive oil
>4 anchovy fillets, coarsely chopped
>2 cloves garlic, crushed
>2 slices (2 oz/50 g) fresh bread (white or brown)
>a little salt

For the broccoli pasta

>1 lb (450 g) broccoli, cut into small pieces
>4 tablespoons (4 × 15 ml spoons) olive oil
>2 cloves garlic, crushed
>1 lb (450 g) quills (or pasta tubes)
>salt and pepper

In a small frying pan gently sauté the garlic and anchovies in the oil until the anchovies begin to disintegrate. Break the bread into small pieces and throw in. Continue to sauté, turning the bread with a spatula until it is crispy. Remove from the heat.

Steam or boil the broccoli until just cooked, but still quite crunchy and green. Drain, and put back into the pan with the oil and garlic. Sauté for a few minutes.

Meanwhile, cook the pasta in plenty of salted, boiling water until 'al dente'. Drain and put into the pan with the broccoli, oil and garlic. Season, and continue cooking for a few minutes.

Quickly reheat the breadcrumbs, taking care not to let them burn, and sprinkle equal portions on each helping of pasta.

Quills with hot lettuce vinaigrette and fried anchovy breadcrumbs

This is an unusual and surprisingly delicate dish – and one of my favourites. I would recommend making the effort to find some really good, tasty lettuce. For example, I have used 6 oz (175 g) curly endive and 2 oz (50 g) of the delicious and beautiful red 'radicchio' lettuce – a good taste and colour combination. You could also try combinations of Belgian endive (sliced), fennel (*very* thinly sliced), cos (sliced) or Chinese cabbage leaves (thinly sliced). And you could throw in a few sprigs of watercress for flavour and colour.

The dish makes an original starter to a dinner party or a tasty main course for two. You don't really need to serve a salad with it!

For 4 starter size helpings, use:

For the hot lettuce vinaigrette

> 6 tablespoons (6 × 15 ml spoons) olive oil
> 1½ tablespoons (1½ × 15 ml spoons) wine vinegar
> 1 teaspoon (1 × 5 ml spoon) French or German mustard
> 1 teaspoon (1 × 5 ml spoon) caster sugar
> salt and pepper
> 8 oz (225 g) lettuce, sliced into strips

For the anchovy breadcrumbs (optional)

> 2 anchovy fillets, coarsely chopped
> 1 slice brown or white bread, lightly toasted and cut into small cubes
> 2 tablespoons (2 × 15 ml spoons) olive oil

Other ingredients

> 8 oz (225 g) quills

Sauté the anchovies in the oil until they begin to disintegrate. Fry the bread cubes in the anchovy oil until they are lightly browned and have absorbed the oil.

Beat the vinaigrette ingredients together in a cup. Season to taste. Sauté the lettuce in the vinaigrette over a gentle heat until the lettuce softens and reduces in size. Season.

Meanwhile, cook the pasta in plenty of salted, boiling water until 'al dente'. Drain, and mix together with the sauce. Sprinkle with the anchovy breadcrumbs (if used) and serve immediately.

Do *not* serve cheese as it will ruin the delicate flavour of the sauce.

ALTERNATIVE VERSION

Omit the anchovy breadcrumbs. Instead, after the lettuce has softened, pour 6 tablespoons (6 × 15 ml spoons) single cream into the pan. Continue cooking until the cream is heated through, then mix the sauce with the pasta cooked 'al dente' as above.

Spaghetti with anchovies, olives, tomatoes and capers

This is a version of a traditional Italian dish known as 'Spaghetti alla putanesca', which translates roughly as 'Roman whore's spaghetti'. Why it is so called I don't know, but certainly the dish *could* be described as spicy and satisfying . . .

This recipe was given to me by Dick Sylbert, the American production designer. After a long and arduous day's filming, Dick would prepare this dish to feed to exhausted and hungry friends – usually a mixture of movie stars and fly fishermen. It always 'hit the spot' as they say!

Again, it is an excellent storecupboard standby, if you can remember to keep a stock of the basic ingredients handy.

For 2 main course helpings use:

> 2 tablespoons (2 × 15 ml spoons) olive oil
> 2 cloves garlic, crushed
> 8 anchovy fillets, coarsely chopped
> up to $\frac{1}{4}$ teaspoon ($\frac{1}{2}$ × 2.5 ml spoon) chilli powder (to taste)
> 16 black olives, halved and pitted
> 1 teaspoon (1 × 5 ml spoon) dried oregano
> 1 tablespoon (1 × 15 ml spoon) capers, drained of vinegar
> salt and pepper
> 12 oz (325–350 g) fresh tomatoes, skinned *or* tinned
>   tomatoes
> 3 tablespoons (3 × 15 ml spoons) fresh chopped herbs (e.g.
>   parsley, basil and coriander, if available)
> 8 oz (225 g) spaghetti (or spaghettini)

Put the oil, crushed garlic and anchovies into a large saucepan and cook over a low heat until the anchovies disintegrate into the oil. Stir in the chilli powder, and then add the olives, dried oregano, capers, seasoning and finally the tomatoes. Simmer over a low heat for 25 minutes, stirring every few minutes and adding some water or chicken stock if the sauce appears to be drying up. Add the fresh herbs (if used) during the cooking.

Meanwhile, cook the pasta in plenty of salted, boiling water. Drain the moment it is 'al dente' and put back into the pan. Pour the sauce on top, and cook for a couple of minutes to allow the pasta to absorb some of the tomato sauce.

Serve very hot.

Twists with anchovies, grilled tomatoes and cream

This is a surprisingly delicate dish in flavour and colour, considering the ingredients used. Excellent for a starter, it can also be served as a main course with a big mixed salad to give the meal colour. Try it also with wholewheat pasta.

For 4 starter size helpings, use:

8 oz (225 g) fresh tomatoes
½ tablespoon (½ × 15 ml spoon) oil
1 teaspoon (1 × 5 ml spoon) dried oregano
3 tablespoons (3 × 15 ml spoons) olive oil
4 anchovy fillets
2 cloves garlic, crushed
8 tablespoons (8 × 15 ml spoons) single cream
8 oz (225 g) twists
salt and pepper

Soak the anchovy fillets in a little milk. Cut the tomatoes in half and sprinkle with the ½ tablespoon oil, the oregano and some salt. Grill until soft. Then skin the halves and chop coarsely.

Chop the anchovies coarsely, and sauté gently with the garlic in the olive oil – taking care not to let the garlic burn – until the anchovies disintegrate. Pour the cream into the pan and continue to cook until the cream begins to bubble. At this point stir in the chopped tomatoes and seasoning.

Meanwhile, cook the pasta in plenty of salted, boiling water until 'al dente'. Drain, and put into the pan containing the sauce. Continue to cook over a gentle heat for a minute or so until the sauce is well mixed with the pasta.

Serve immediately, *without* putting grated cheese on the table. Cheese would spoil the delicate taste of this dish.

Spaghettini with red caviar

This recipe was invented by culinary expert *extraordinaire*, Loyd Grossman, for his book *The Millionaire's Diet Book* (Macdonald).

The red caviar is in fact red salmon roe, and is not to be confused with the orange-red lumpfish roe, a vastly inferior (although considerably cheaper) product. The dish is delicious, unashamedly luxurious, non-fattening, and simplicity itself to prepare – well worth the extra expense and the trouble finding a shop which sells the stuff!

Loyd recommends using one of the finer spaghettis, such as spaghettini or vermicelli.

For 4 starter or small main course helpings, use:

> 4 oz (100–125 g) salmon roe (we use a brand called Keta)
> ½ oz (15 g) butter
> 10 oz (275 g) spaghettini (or thin spaghetti)

Cook the pasta in plenty of salted, boiling water until 'al dente'. Drain, and put into a preheated serving dish with the butter. When the butter has melted, gently stir in the 'caviar' (salmon roe), using a wooden spoon.

Serve immediately.

Spaghetti with lightly curried prawns and cream

For 4 main course helpings, use:

1 oz (25 g) butter
1 clove garlic, crushed
4 oz (100–125 g) onion, finely sliced
1½ teaspoons (3 × 2.5 ml spoons) curry powder (to taste)
1 wine glass (4 fl oz/125 ml) white wine
1 tablespoon (1 × 15 ml spoon) flour
¼ pint (150 ml) milk
8 oz (225 g) prawns, cooked and shelled (frozen do very
    well)
3 tablespoons (3 × 15 ml spoons) double cream
1 lb (450 g) spaghetti (or small macaroni)

Melt the butter in a covered pan. Add the garlic and onion, and stew on a very low heat until the onion is well softened. Mix in the curry powder, half the wine, and then the flour, stirring thoroughly. After a minute, start adding the milk little by little – stirring all the time – and then the rest of the wine. As soon as you have a smooth sauce, add the prawns and bring to the boil. *Immediately* the sauce boils, remove it from the heat and allow to cool. Add the cream and the seasoning. Reheat just before adding to the pasta.

Cook the pasta in plenty of salted, boiling water until 'al dente'. Drain, and return it to the pan or to a preheated serving dish. Pour in the sauce and mix it with the pasta using two wooden spoons.

Serve immediately.

Twists with crab cream sauce

As this delicately flavoured cream sauce is almost white in colour it is a good idea to serve it on one of the coloured pasta, either wholewheat or one of the green or pink varieties. The prettiest are the packets of three colours together, red, green and white.

For 3–4 main course helpings, use:

>1 oz (25 g) butter
>1–2 cloves garlic, crushed
>6 oz (175 g) tin crabmeat
>½ wine glass (2 fl oz/50 ml) white wine
>½ pint (275 ml) single cream
>salt and pepper
>10–14 oz (275–400 g) twists (or another pasta shape)
>freshly grated Parmesan cheese (optional)

Melt the butter in a heavy-bottomed pan large enough to take the cooked pasta and sauce. Add the garlic and sauté gently until it begins to turn golden. Quickly add the crabmeat and stir, breaking up the lumps with a wooden spoon. Add the white wine and allow it to bubble for a minute or so. Stir in the cream and season to taste. Cook on a very low heat (taking care not to let the mixture boil) for about 10 minutes, to allow the crab flavour to infuse the cream.

Meanwhile, cook the pasta in plenty of salted, boiling water. Remove from the heat while still only just 'al dente', and drain. Add the pasta to the pot containing the cream sauce, and continue cooking very gently, turning continuously with the wooden spoon to enable the pasta to absorb some of the cream sauce.

Serve with freshly grated Parmesan on the side (if you like) and with plenty of freshly ground black pepper.

Quills with crab, parsley, mushrooms and cream

For 2 main course helpings, use:

½ oz (15 g) butter
4 oz (100–125 g) mushrooms, sliced
1 tablespoon (1 × 15 ml spoon) olive oil
1–2 cloves garlic, crushed
1–2 pinches chilli powder or paprika pepper
7 oz (200 g) tin crabmeat
½ wine glass (2 fl oz/50 ml) white wine
3 tablespoons (3 × 15 ml spoons) double cream
salt and pepper
1 tablespoon (1 × 15 ml spoon) fresh, chopped parsley
8 oz (225 g) quills

Sauté the mushrooms in the butter until they soften and begin to darken. Put aside.

Sauté the garlic in the oil in a large frying pan, stirring for just a minute over a low heat and taking care not to let the garlic burn. Stir in the chilli powder and then add the crab, breaking it up with a wooden spoon. Stir in the wine and the cooked mushrooms, and allow the mixture to bubble for a minute or so to reduce the liquid a little. Add the cream, seasoning and parsley, and cook for another couple of minutes.

Meanwhile, cook the pasta in plenty of salted, boiling water. Remove from the heat and drain the moment the pasta is 'al dente'. Return the pasta to the pan. Pour on the sauce, and continue cooking over a low heat, stirring continuously, to allow the pasta to absorb some of the sauce.

Serve very hot.

Frank's spaghetti vongole

For 4 main course helpings, use:

1 oz (25 g) butter
1 tablespoon (1 × 15 ml spoon) oil
4 oz (100–125 g) onion, finely sliced (if possible use the dark red onions)
5 cloves garlic, crushed
16–20 oz (450–575 g) tinned baby clams
1 wine glass (4 fl oz/125 ml) white wine
1 oz (25 g) fresh chopped parsley
salt and pepper
1 lb (450 g) spaghetti (or spaghettini)

Melt the butter with the oil in a large frying pan or saucepan. Add the onions and garlic and sauté until the onions are translucent. Stir in the clam juice and the wine, and boil briskly until the liquid has reduced by about half. Add the clams and heat through for another couple of minutes. The parsley and seasoning should be added to the sauce at the last minute.

Meanwhile, cook the pasta in plenty of salted, boiling water. Drain and put into a preheated serving dish. Mix the sauce well into the pasta.

Serve immediately.

Spaghetti with clams and tomato sauce

This recipe is less complicated than might appear at first glance. Spaghetti with clams and tomato sauce is a popular and very traditional Italian dish. In Italy you might be lucky enough to be served 'Spaghetti con vongole e sugo', with fresh clams still in their shells. My version, consisting as it does of ingredients that can be kept in the store cupboard, is infinitely more practical and convenient for the English cook but still *very* delicious – highly recommended!

There are many variations you can try: you could use more or less clams depending on availability and price, throw in herbs according to taste, leave out the onions if you don't happen to have any. You could make a spicier version by adding chilli powder, or ½–1 small dried chilli, de-seeded and chopped, and 2–3 coarsely chopped anchovy fillets. Any additional ingredients should be stirred in while you sauté the onion and garlic.

Served with a big, green, crisp salad, this is a satisfying meal in itself.

For 3–4 main course helpings, use:

> 3 tablespoons (3 × 15 ml spoons) olive oil
> 4 oz (100–125 g) onions, chopped
> 2 cloves garlic, crushed
> 1 medium tin clams (7–10 oz/200–275 g) *or* 2 small jars (3½ oz/100 g each) Italian clams, shelled
> 2 × 14 oz (2 × 400 g) tins tomatoes
> 2 tablespoons (2 × 15 ml spoons) tomato purée
> 1½ teaspoons (1½ × 5 ml spoons) sugar (optional)
> 1 wine glass (4 fl oz/125 ml) white wine (optional)
> 2 bay leaves (optional)
> salt and pepper
> 2 teaspoons (2 × 5 ml spoons) dried herbs (e.g. oregano or sage)
> 12–16 oz (325–450 g) spaghetti (or spaghettini)

Sauté the onion and garlic in the oil over a low heat for several minutes until the onion is translucent. Add the juice from the clams, and then the tomatoes, tomato purée, sugar, white wine, bay leaves and seasoning. Break up the tomatoes a little with a wooden spoon, and then simmer in a covered pan for about 25 minutes, stirring frequently. Add the herbs after about 15 minutes. Just before adding the sauce to the pasta, add the clams and heat through thoroughly.

Meanwhile, cook the pasta in plenty of salted, boiling water until 'al dente'. Drain and put back into the pan or into a preheated serving dish. Add the sauce and mix together well.

Serve very hot without Parmesan cheese but with plenty of freshly ground black pepper.

Spaghetti with pepper and clams – 'Gary Cooper'

This recipe was given to me by Tessa Dahl Kelly. It was handed down to her by her mother, the film actress Patricia Neal, who used to feed it to Gary Cooper during their well-publicized liaison.

(The original recipe suggests green peppers, but I think the dish is more colourful and tasty if you use more than one colour. Use whatever you can find!)

For 6 starter size helpings, use:

> 5 tablespoons (5 × 15 ml spoons) olive oil
> 2 cloves garlic, crushed
> 4 oz (100–125 g) onion, finely chopped
> 6 oz (175 g) red, green and yellow peppers, very finely chopped
> 2 tablespoons (2 × 15 ml spoons) plain flour
> 14 oz (400 g) tinned clams (in brine)
> 6 tablespoons (6 × 15 ml spoons) chopped fresh parsley
> $\frac{1}{2}$ tablespoon ($\frac{1}{2}$ × 15 ml spoon) dried thyme
> white wine or tomato juice (if needed, to thin the sauce)
> 12 oz (325–350 g) spaghetti or quills

Sauté the garlic, onion and peppers together in the oil for a few minutes until softened. Stir in the flour, then add the clams with the brine and the herbs. Cover and simmer for 15 minutes. Stir frequently, and if the sauce appears too thick, add some white wine or tomato juice.

Meanwhile, cook the pasta in plenty of salted, boiling water until 'al dente'. Drain, and mix in well with the hot sauce.

Serve immediately from a preheated serving dish.

Tagliatelle with mussels, cream and Dijon mustard

This recipe was suggested to me by the chef at a charming little lunch place in Los Angeles called Hugo's. Hugo's used to be a butcher's shop selling reputedly the best veal in L.A. Half the premises is still given over to the selling of meat from behind glass, while the other half feeds the glamorous *jeunesse d'or* of Beverly Hills – for, surprisingly, very reasonable prices. Tousle-haired young movie actors ostentatiously flick through scripts while nibbling at their pasta and salad and are almost indistinguishable from the serving staff which consists largely of resting thespians. 'Big talk' – deals and dollars – resonates through the air as struggling directors lunch with aspiring producers.

The original recipe called for fresh wild mushrooms and fresh mussels. Being too lazy to prepare the mussels, and having no idea how to obtain fresh wild mushrooms, I have used ordinary mushrooms and tinned mussels. The result is still perfectly delicious.

For 4 starter or 2 main course helpings, use:

> 1 oz (25 g) butter
> 1 clove garlic, crushed
> 2 oz (50 g) onions or shallots, finely chopped
> 4 oz (100–125 g) mushrooms, sliced
> *8 oz (225 g) tinned mussels
> 1 wine glass (4 fl oz/125 ml) white wine
> 1 tablespoon (1 × 15 ml spoon) chopped fresh parsley
> 1 generous teaspoon (1 × 5 ml spoon) Dijon mustard
> ¼ pint (150 ml) double cream
> 8–10 oz (225–275 g) tagliatelle (or other pasta)

Melt the butter in a heavy-bottomed saucepan large enough to hold the finished pasta and sauce. Sauté the garlic and onions until the onions become translucent. Add the mushrooms and

* Do *not* use mussels prepared in vinegar

cook for about 4 minutes until they soften and darken. Stir in the mussels, the white wine and the parsley and bring to the boil for a minute or so. Lower the heat and carefully stir in the mustard so that it is well integrated. Add the double cream, and continue cooking on a low heat for 2–3 minutes.

Cook the pasta in plenty of salted, boiling water until 'al dente'. Drain, and add the pasta to the pan containing the sauce. Continue cooking on a low heat, stirring continuously, until the pasta has absorbed some of the sauce and all the ingredients are piping hot.

Serve immediately.

Note: If the sauce sits for any length of time, while the pasta is cooking, it may thicken slightly. Add some extra single cream, or double cream mixed with milk, before mixing with the pasta.

Linguine with scallops, mushrooms, cream and wine

This dish is starter, fish, vegetable and pudding courses all rolled into one. It is a real treat, containing particularly luxurious and spoiling ingredients.

For 2 main course helpings, use:

1 oz (25 g) butter
1 clove garlic, sliced
4–6 oz (100–175 g) scallops (with or without coral), sliced
6 oz (175 g) broccoli, sliced into smallish pieces
1 wineglass (4 fl oz/125 ml) white wine
4 oz (100–125 g) mushrooms, sliced
$\frac{3}{4}$ pint (425 ml) single cream
$\frac{1}{2}$ teaspoon (1 × 2.5 ml spoon) Dijon mustard
salt and pepper
8 oz (225 g) linguine (or another pasta)

In a medium-sized, covered pan, sauté the garlic in half the butter over a low heat. Add the scallops and sauté or stir-fry for a couple of minutes, turning continuously with a wooden spatula or spoon. Add the broccoli and continue to sauté or stir-fry, turning with the wooden spoon for another 2–3 minutes. Pour in the wine, cover, and leave the ingredients to steam in the wine and juice for the next 10–12 minutes. Check occasionally that the liquid hasn't dried up entirely, and give the mixture a little stir. If it looks *too* dry, add a little more wine or water. Add the sliced mushrooms, the cream and the mustard, and continue to cook, stirring occasionally, for another 3–4 minutes. Season.

Meanwhile, cook the pasta in plenty of salted, boiling water until 'al dente'. Add the remaining butter to the drained pasta, pour on the sauce and stir over gentle heat until it is well mixed with the pasta and thoroughly heated through.

Serve immediately – with extra Parmesan cheese on the side only if you must. It doesn't need it!

Rosemary's shells with scallops, cream and curry

A delicious and luxurious dish that is very simple and quick to make. It is excellent as a starter for a dinner party, or as a quick supper for two. (Instead of using scallops only, you could use a combination of scallops and prawns or shrimps.)

For 4 starter size helpings, use:

1 oz (25 g) butter
6 oz (175 g) scallops (with or without coral), cut into small
    pieces
½–¾ teaspoon (½–¾ × 5 ml spoon) curry powder
1 wine glass (4 fl oz/125 ml) white wine
¼ pint (150 ml) double cream
salt and pepper
8 oz (225 g) shells

Melt the butter in a large frying pan and gently sauté the scallops for 3–4 minutes. Stir in the curry powder. Add the wine, and allow to bubble until the liquid has reduced by about half. Then stir in the cream.

Meanwhile, cook the pasta in plenty of salted, boiling water until only just 'al dente'. Remove quickly from the heat, drain, and put into the pan with the sauce. Continue cooking the pasta and sauce over a low heat, stirring with a wooden spoon, until the pasta is fully cooked and has absorbed some of the liquid from the sauce.

Serve immediately, with ground black pepper but *no* cheese!

Recipe for béchamel sauce

Béchamel sauce is used in a number of the recipes. To make the sauce, use the quantities specified for the recipe you are following, and proceed as follows:

VERSION 1

Put the milk into a pan with 2 bay leaves, half an onion and a few peppercorns. Bring to just below the boil, then remove from the heat and leave to infuse for 15 minutes. Strain.

Melt the butter slowly in a heavy-bottomed pan, taking care not to let it burn. Mix in the flour, stirring well with a wooden spoon. Add the milk, a little at a time, stirring constantly until the lumps disappear and the sauce thickens. If the sauce ingredients include mustard powder and/or grated cheese, stir them in when you have used up all the milk.

VERSION 2 (A QUICKER METHOD)

If you are in a hurry, proceed as above, but omit the bay leaves, onion and peppercorns and use milk straight from the bottle or carton.

Note: If the sauce develops lumps, beat it with an egg whisk or electric hand beater. I usually whisk it anyway, for good measure!

Index

Main ingredients are indicated by **bold** type

147